STAR WARS®

THE OLD REPUBLIC™

VOLUME TWO
THREAT OF PEACE

THE OLD REPUBLIC

(25,000–1,000 YEARS BEFORE THE BATTLE OF YAVIN)

The Old Republic was the legendary government that united a galaxy under the rule of the Senate. In this era, the Jedi are numerous, and serve as guardians of peace and justice. *The Old Republic* comics series takes place in this era, chronicling the immense wars fought by the Jedi of old, and the ancient Sith.

The events in these stories take place approximately 3,600 years before the Battle of Yavin.

STAR WARS
THE OLD REPUBLIC

VOLUME TWO
THREAT OF PEACE

SCRIPT
ROB CHESTNEY

ART
ALEX SANCHEZ

COLORS
MICHAEL ATIYEH

LETTERING
MICHAEL HEISLER

FRONT COVER ART
BENJAMIN CARRÉ

PRESIDENT AND PUBLISHER
MIKE RICHARDSON

COLLECTION DESIGNER
STEPHEN REICHERT

ASSISTANT EDITOR
FREDDYE LINS

EDITOR
DAVE MARSHALL

Special thanks to Daniel Erickson, Alexander Freed, Hall Hood, Deborah Shin, and Leo Olebe at BioWare; Stephen Ervin and Rob Cowles at LucasArts; and Jann Moorhead, David Anderman, Troy Alders, Leland Chee, Frank Parisi, Sue Rostoni, and Carol Roeder at Lucas Licensing.

EXECUTIVE VICE PRESIDENT **NEIL HANKERSON** · CHIEF FINANCIAL OFFICER **TOM WEDDLE** · VICE PRESIDENT OF PUBLISHING **RANDY STRADLEY** · VICE PRESIDENT OF BUSINESS DEVELOPMENT **MICHAEL MARTENS** · VICE PRESIDENT OF BUSINESS AFFAIRS **ANITA NELSON** · VICE PRESIDENT OF MARKETING **MICHA HERSHMAN** · VICE PRESIDENT OF PRODUCT DEVELOPMENT **DAVID SCROGGY** · VICE PRESIDENT OF INFORMATION TECHNOLOGY **DALE LAFOUNTAIN** · DIRECTOR OF PURCHASING **DARLENE VOGEL** · GENERAL COUNSEL **KEN LIZZI** · EDITORIAL DIRECTOR **DAVEY ESTRADA** · SENIOR MANAGING EDITOR **SCOTT ALLIE** · SENIOR BOOKS EDITOR **CHRIS WARNER** · EXECUTIVE EDITOR **DIANA SCHUTZ** · DIRECTOR OF DESIGN AND PRODUCTION **CARY GRAZZINI** · ART DIRECTOR **LIA RIBACCHI** · DIRECTOR OF SCHEDULING **CARA NIECE**

STAR WARS: THE OLD REPUBLIC • Volume 2—THREAT OF PEACE

This volume collects issues #1 through #27 of the series *Star Wars:* The Old Republic, which originally appeared on StarWarsTheOldRepublic.com.

Published by
Dark Horse Books
A division of Dark Horse Comics, Inc.
10956 SE Main Street
Milwaukie, OR 97222

DarkHorse.com | StarWars.com

To find a comics shop in your area, call the Comic Shop Locator Service toll-free at 1-888-266-4226

Library of Congress Cataloging-in-Publication Data

Chestney, Robert.
Threat of peace / script, Rob Chestney ; art, Alex Sanchez ; colors, Michael Atiyeh ; lettering, Michael Heisler ; front cover art, Benjamin Carré.
p. cm. -- (Star Wars: The old republic ; v. 2)
Summary: As representatives of the Galactic Republic and the Sith Empire attempt to negotiate a peace treaty, deception by the Sith puts the Jedi in an unfortunate position.
ISBN 978-1-59582-642-8
1. Graphic novels. [1. Graphic novels. 2. Science fiction.] I. Sanchez, Alex, ill. II. Heisler, Michael. III. Carr, Benjamin. IV. Title.
PZ7.7.C43Thr 2011
741.5--dc22
[Fic]
2010046434

First edition: May 2011
ISBN 978-1-59582-642-8

3 5 7 9 10 8 6 4 2
Printed at Midas Printing International, Ltd., Huizhou, China

THREAT OF PEACE

After centuries of exile in deep space, the true Sith Empire has returned to the galaxy to exact its vengeance on the Galactic Republic.

Spread out across several star systems, Republic military forces and members of the Jedi Order have fought bravely to slow the Empire's advances.

To end the stalemate, the Lords of the Sith Dark Council have extended an offer to the Galactic Senate to engage in cease-fire talks. Wary but desperate, Republic and Jedi leaders have agreed to meet the Sith on Alderaan.

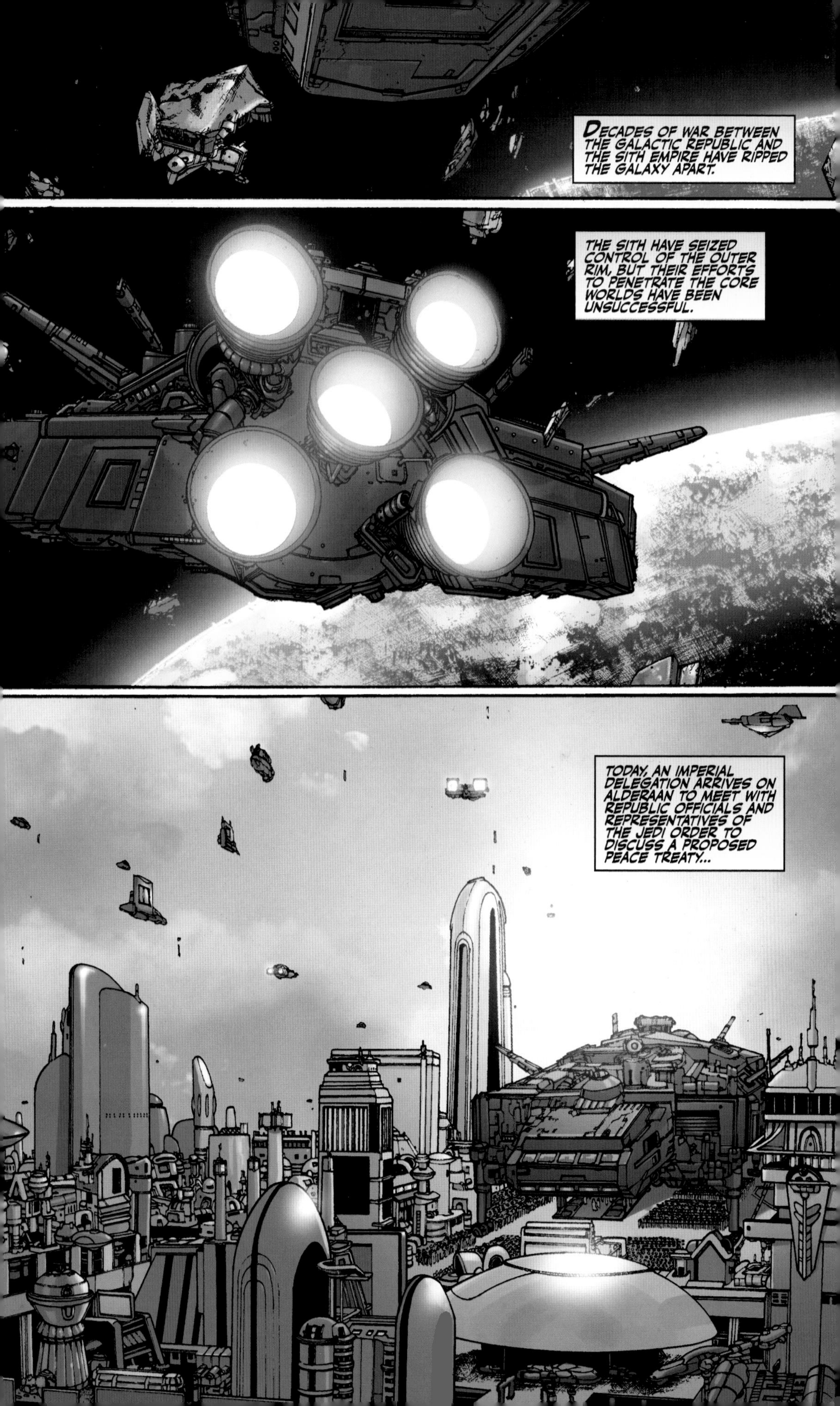
DECADES OF WAR BETWEEN THE GALACTIC REPUBLIC AND THE SITH EMPIRE HAVE RIPPED THE GALAXY APART.
THE SITH HAVE SEIZED CONTROL OF THE OUTER RIM, BUT THEIR EFFORTS TO PENETRATE THE CORE WORLDS HAVE BEEN UNSUCCESSFUL.
TODAY, AN IMPERIAL DELEGATION ARRIVES ON ALDERAAN TO MEET WITH REPUBLIC OFFICIALS AND REPRESENTATIVES OF THE JEDI ORDER TO DISCUSS A PROPOSED PEACE TREATY...

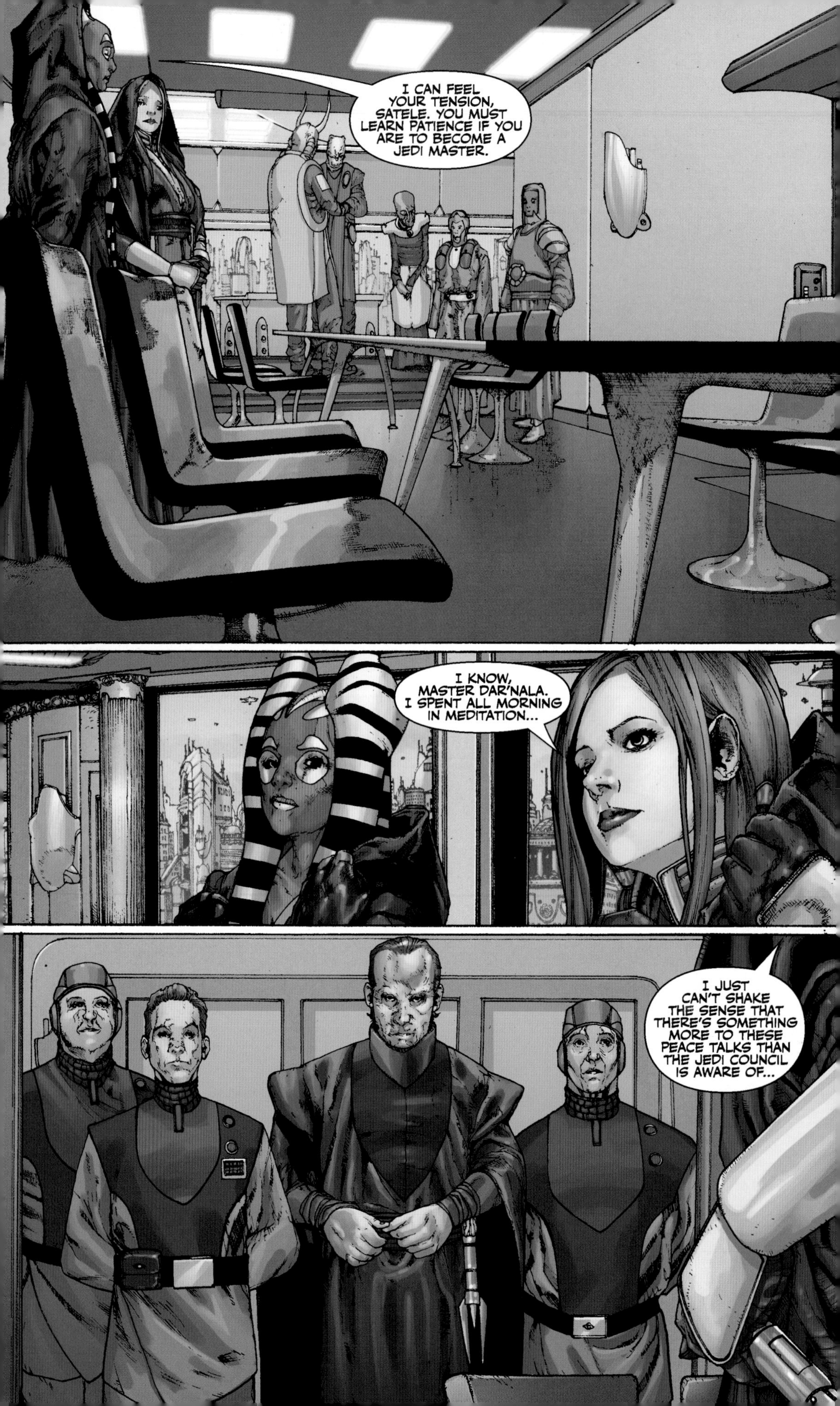
I CAN FEEL YOUR TENSION, SATELE. YOU MUST LEARN PATIENCE IF YOU ARE TO BECOME A JEDI MASTER.
I KNOW, MASTER DAR'NALA. I SPENT ALL MORNING IN MEDITATION...
I JUST CAN'T SHAKE THE SENSE THAT THERE'S SOMETHING MORE TO THESE PEACE TALKS THAN THE JEDI COUNCIL IS AWARE OF...

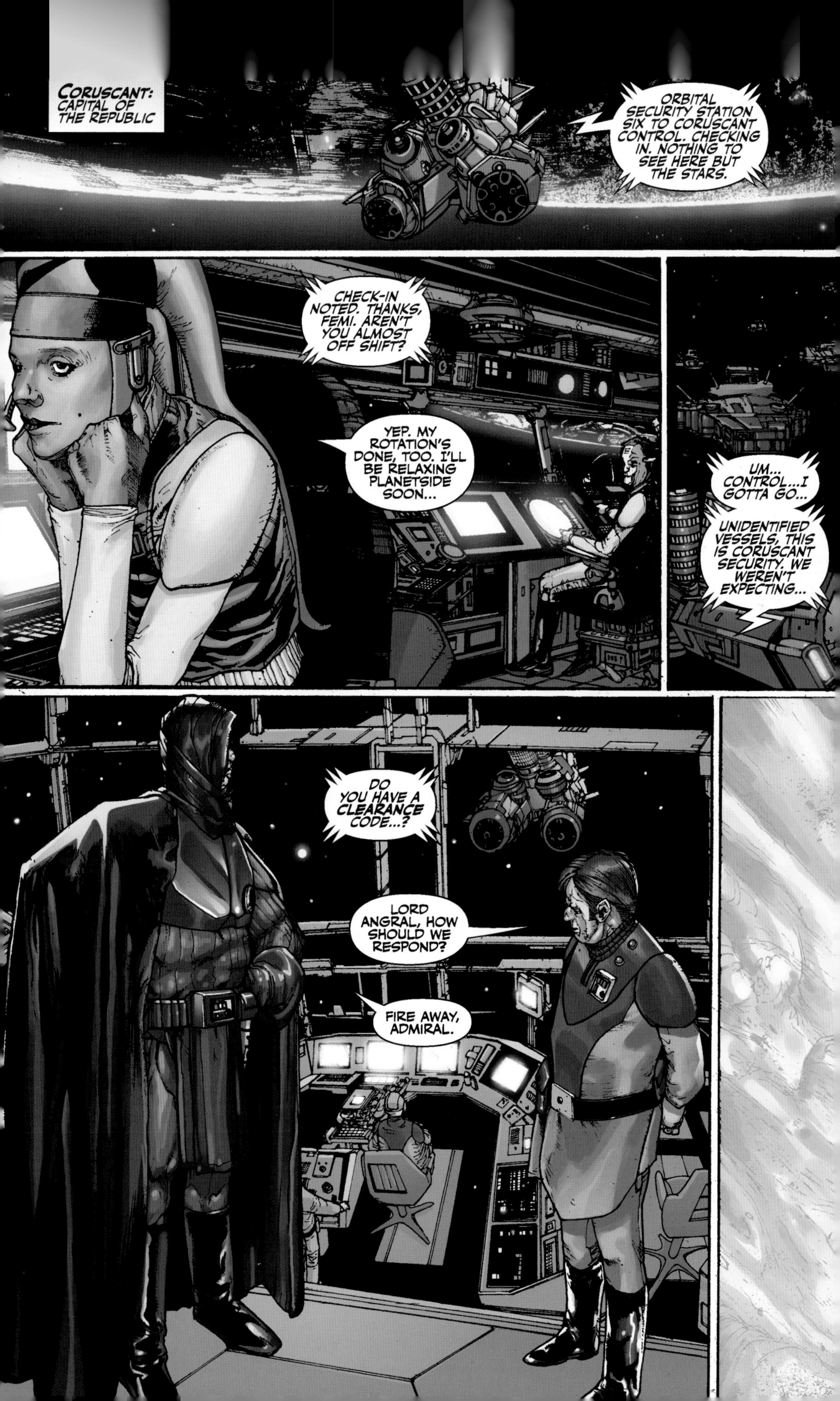
CORUSCANT: CAPITAL OF THE REPUBLIC
ORBITAL SECURITY STATION SIX TO CORUSCANT CONTROL. CHECKING IN. NOTHING TO SEE HERE BUT THE STARS.
CHECK-IN NOTED. THANKS, FEMI. AREN'T YOU ALMOST OFF SHIFT?
YEP. MY ROTATION'S DONE, TOO. I'LL BE RELAXING PLANETSIDE SOON...
UM... CONTROL...I GOTTA GO...
UNIDENTIFIED VESSELS, THIS IS CORUSCANT SECURITY. WE WEREN'T EXPECTING...
DO YOU HAVE A CLEARANCE CODE...?
LORD ANGRAL, HOW SHOULD WE RESPOND?
FIRE AWAY, ADMIRAL.

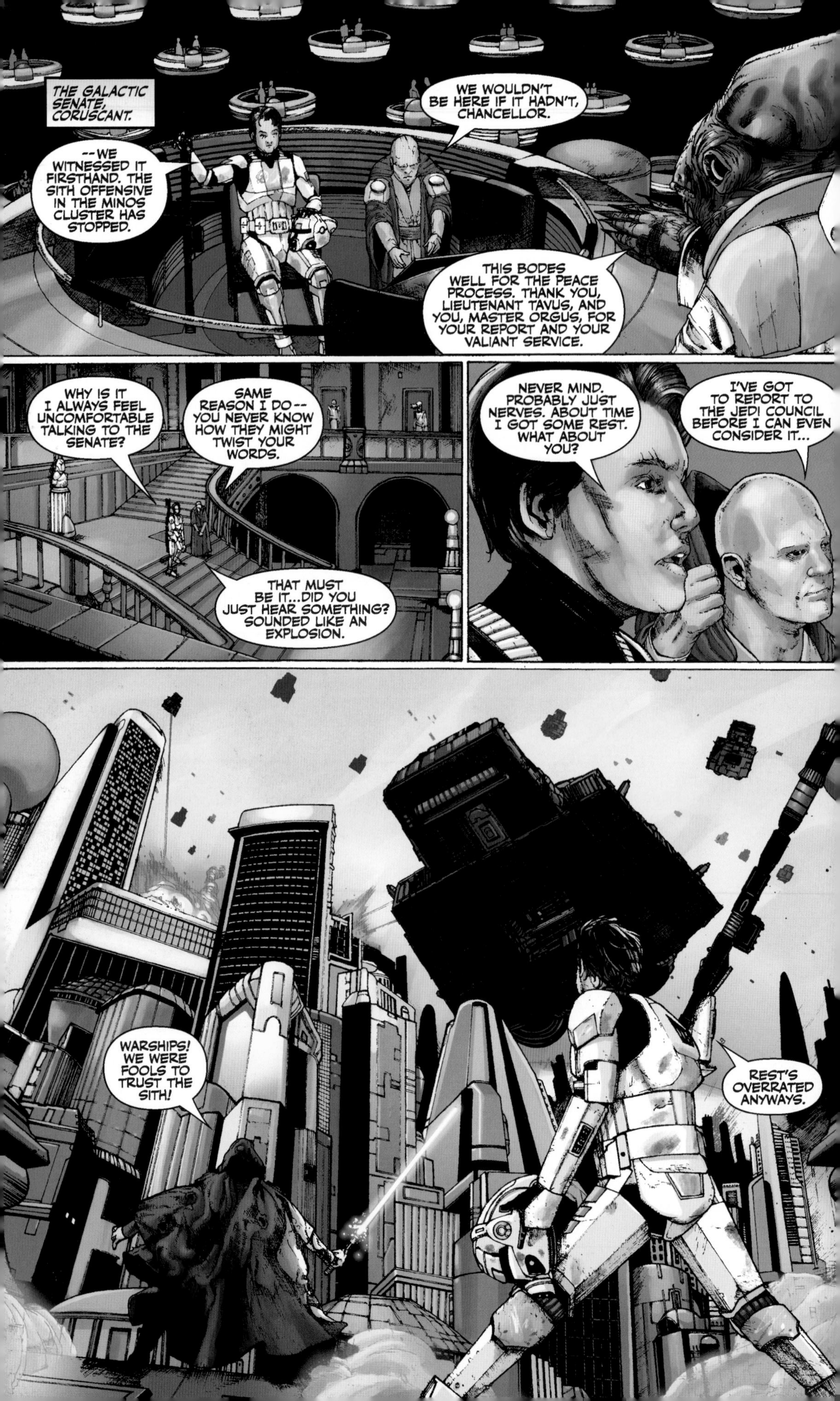

THE GALACTIC SENATE, CORUSCANT.
--WE WITNESSED IT FIRSTHAND. THE SITH OFFENSIVE IN THE MINOS CLUSTER HAS STOPPED.
WE WOULDN'T BE HERE IF IT HADN'T, CHANCELLOR.
THIS BODES WELL FOR THE PEACE PROCESS. THANK YOU, LIEUTENANT TAVUS, AND YOU, MASTER ORGUS, FOR YOUR REPORT AND YOUR VALIANT SERVICE.
WHY IS IT I ALWAYS FEEL UNCOMFORTABLE TALKING TO THE SENATE?
SAME REASON I DO-- YOU NEVER KNOW HOW THEY MIGHT TWIST YOUR WORDS.
THAT MUST BE IT...DID YOU JUST HEAR SOMETHING? SOUNDED LIKE AN EXPLOSION.
NEVER MIND. PROBABLY JUST NERVES. ABOUT TIME I GOT SOME REST. WHAT ABOUT YOU?
I'VE GOT TO REPORT TO THE JEDI COUNCIL BEFORE I CAN EVEN CONSIDER IT...
WARSHIPS! WE WERE FOOLS TO TRUST THE SITH!
REST'S OVERRATED ANYWAYS.

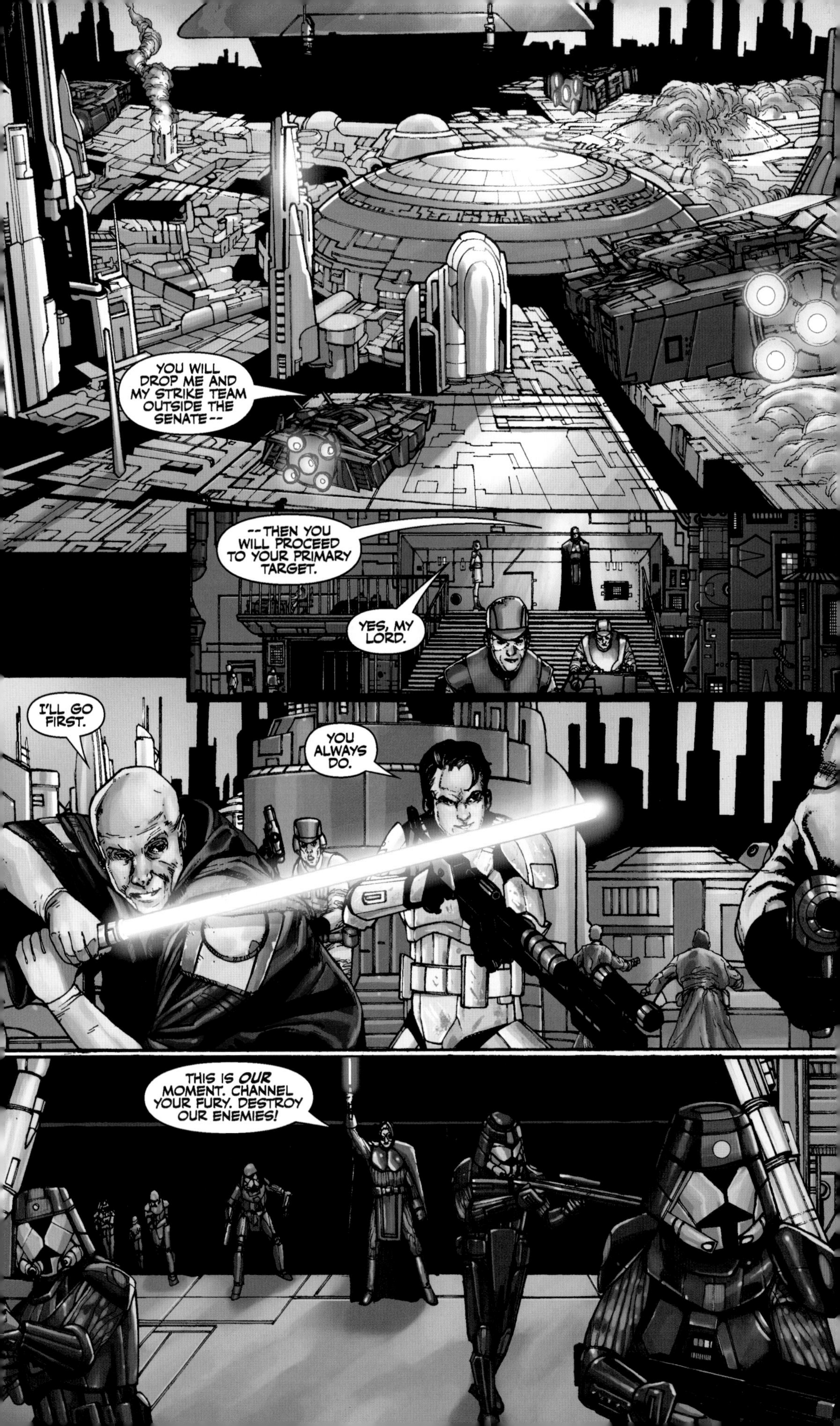
YOU WILL DROP ME AND MY STRIKE TEAM OUTSIDE THE SENATE--
--THEN YOU WILL PROCEED TO YOUR PRIMARY TARGET.
YES, MY LORD.
I'LL GO FIRST.
YOU ALWAYS DO.
THIS IS *OUR* MOMENT. CHANNEL YOUR FURY. DESTROY OUR ENEMIES!

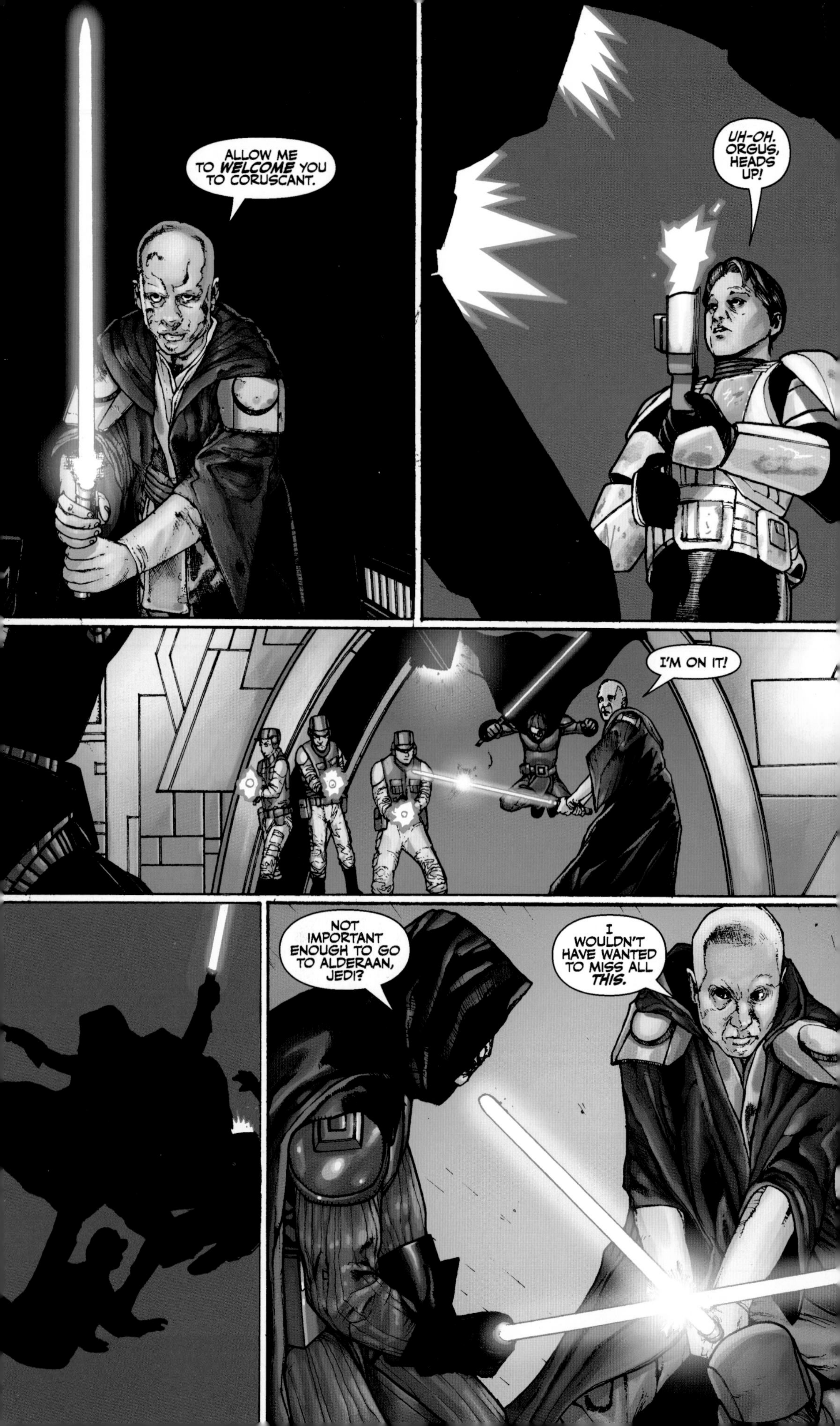
ALLOW ME TO WELCOME YOU TO CORUSCANT.
UH-OH. ORGUS, HEADS UP!
I'M ON IT!
NOT IMPORTANT ENOUGH TO GO TO ALDERAAN, JEDI?
I WOULDN'T HAVE WANTED TO MISS ALL THIS.

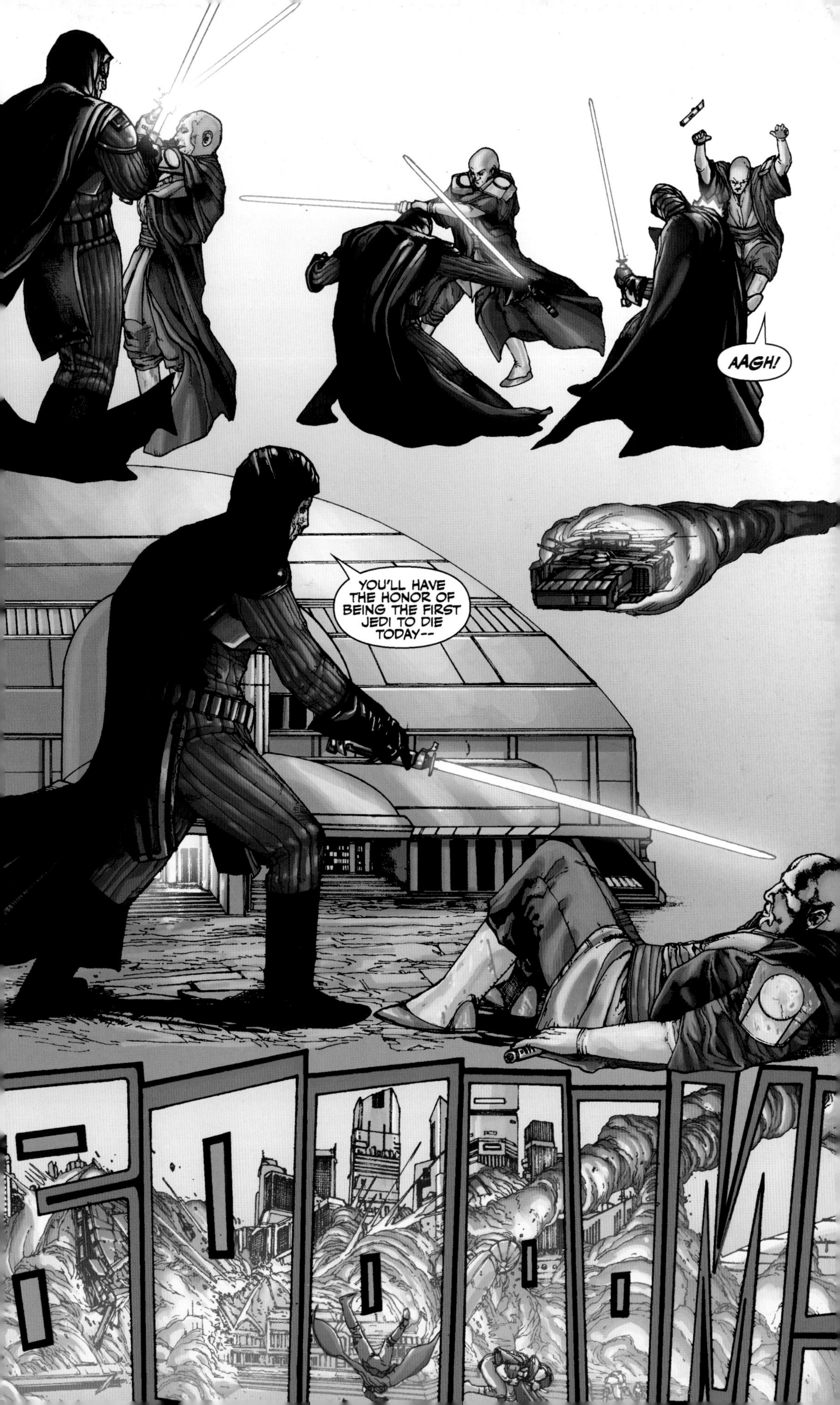
AAGH!
YOU'LL HAVE THE HONOR OF BEING THE FIRST JEDI TO DIE TODAY--

WHOOAH...
WH-WHAT WAS
THAT...? ORGUS?

THE JEDI
TEMPLE!
ORGUS!

HEARD YOU
THE FIRST TIME...
I'M COMING.

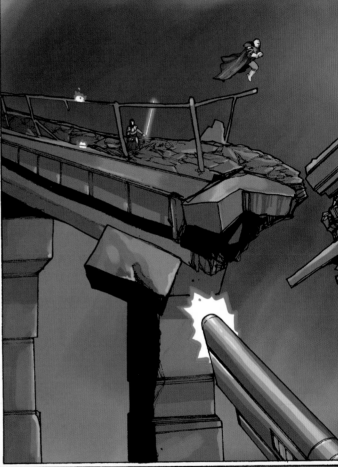

COWARDS.
LET THEM GO.
OUR BUSINESS IS
IN THE SENATE
TOWER.

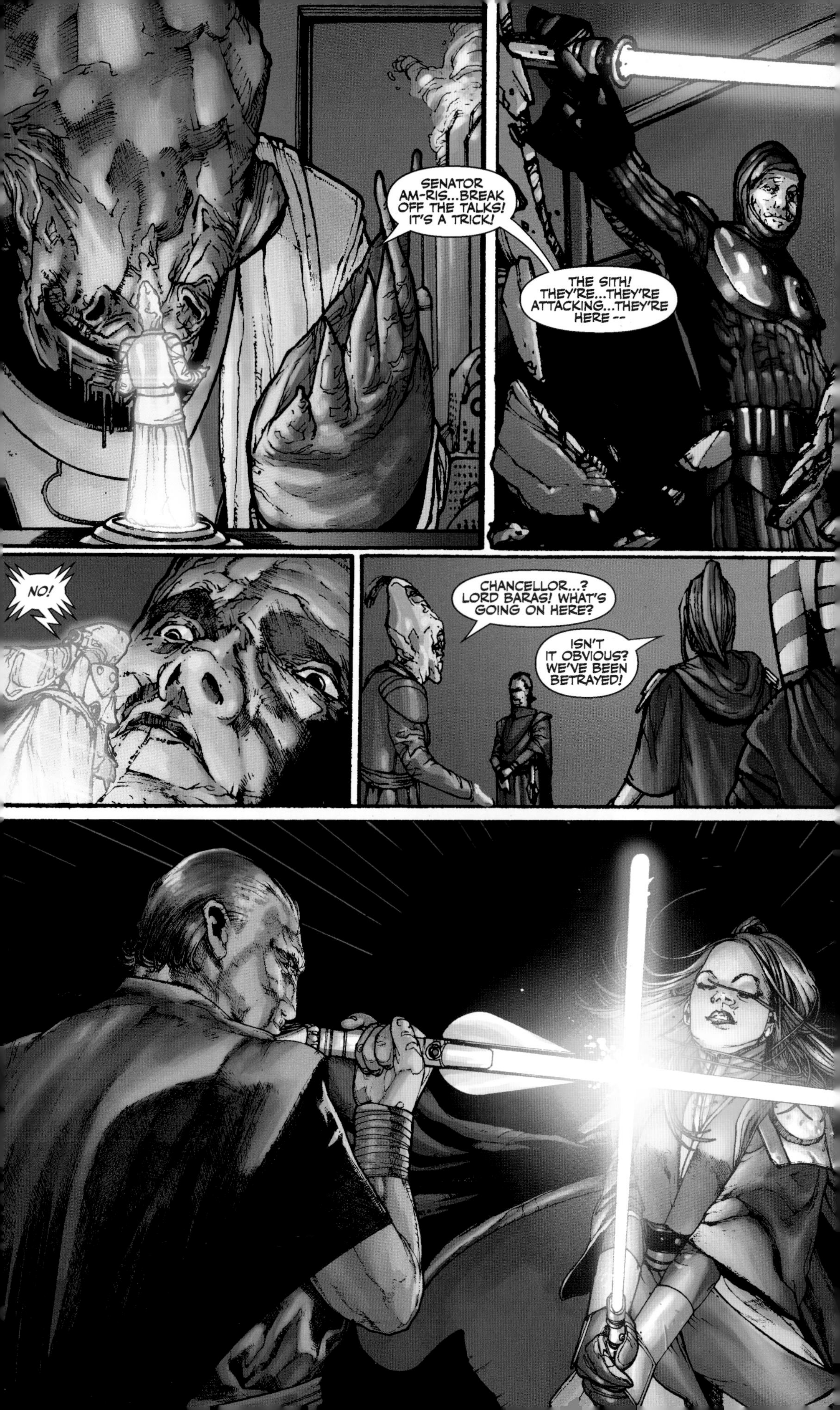
SENATOR AM-RIS...BREAK OFF THE TALKS! IT'S A TRICK!
THE SITH! THEY'RE...THEY'RE ATTACKING...THEY'RE HERE --
NO!
CHANCELLOR...? LORD BARAS! WHAT'S GOING ON HERE?
ISN'T IT OBVIOUS? WE'VE BEEN BETRAYED!

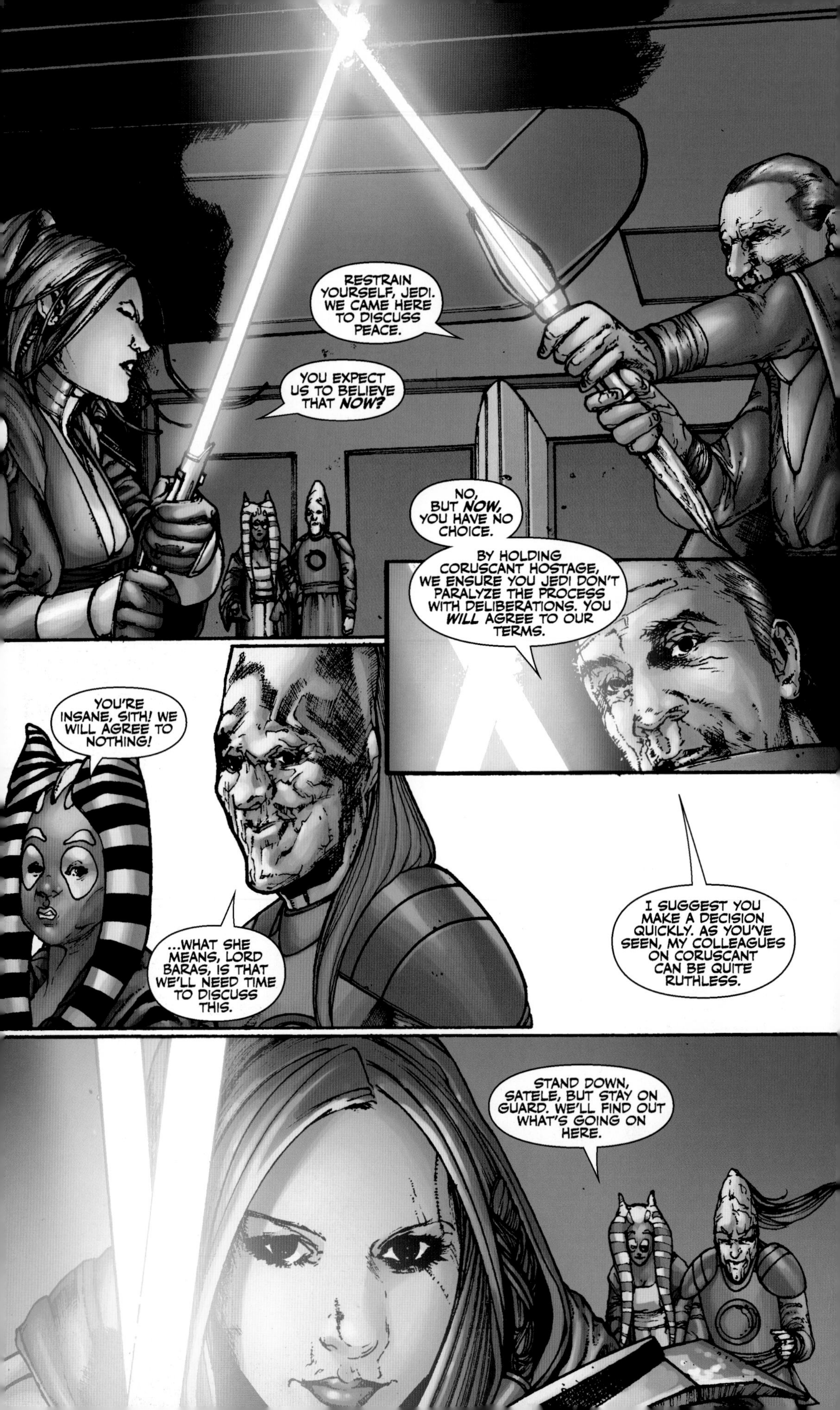
RESTRAIN YOURSELF, JEDI. WE CAME HERE TO DISCUSS PEACE.
YOU EXPECT US TO BELIEVE THAT *NOW?*
NO, BUT *NOW,* YOU HAVE NO CHOICE.
BY HOLDING CORUSCANT HOSTAGE, WE ENSURE YOU JEDI DON'T PARALYZE THE PROCESS WITH DELIBERATIONS. YOU *WILL* AGREE TO OUR TERMS.
YOU'RE INSANE, SITH! WE WILL AGREE TO NOTHING!
...WHAT SHE MEANS, LORD BARAS, IS THAT WE'LL NEED TIME TO DISCUSS THIS.
I SUGGEST YOU MAKE A DECISION QUICKLY. AS YOU'VE SEEN, MY COLLEAGUES ON CORUSCANT CAN BE QUITE RUTHLESS.
STAND DOWN, SATELE, BUT STAY ON GUARD. WE'LL FIND OUT WHAT'S GOING ON HERE.

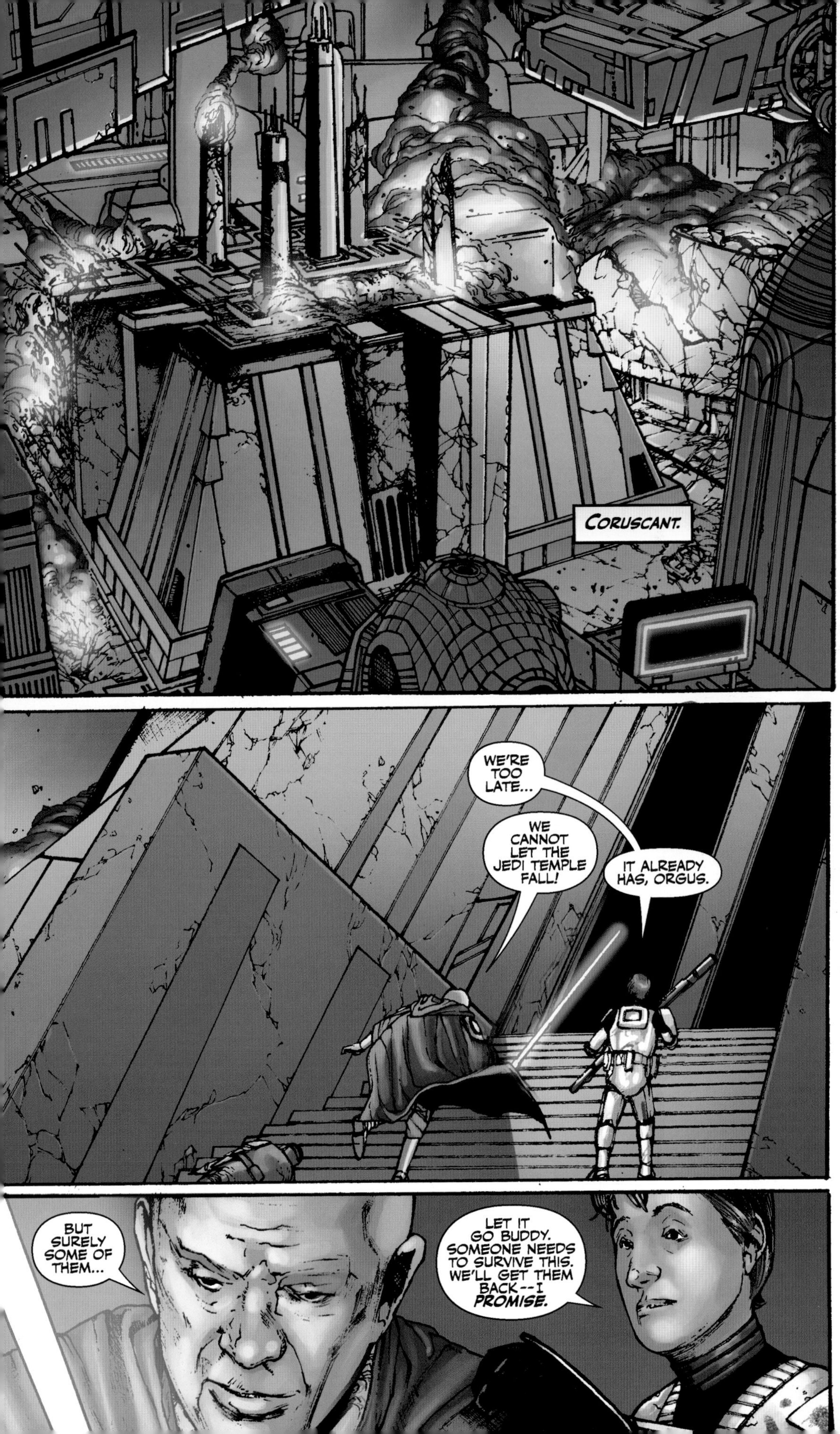
CORUSCANT.
WE'RE TOO LATE...
WE CANNOT LET THE JEDI TEMPLE FALL!
IT ALREADY HAS, ORGUS.
BUT SURELY SOME OF THEM...
LET IT GO BUDDY. SOMEONE NEEDS TO SURVIVE THIS. WE'LL GET THEM BACK--I PROMISE.

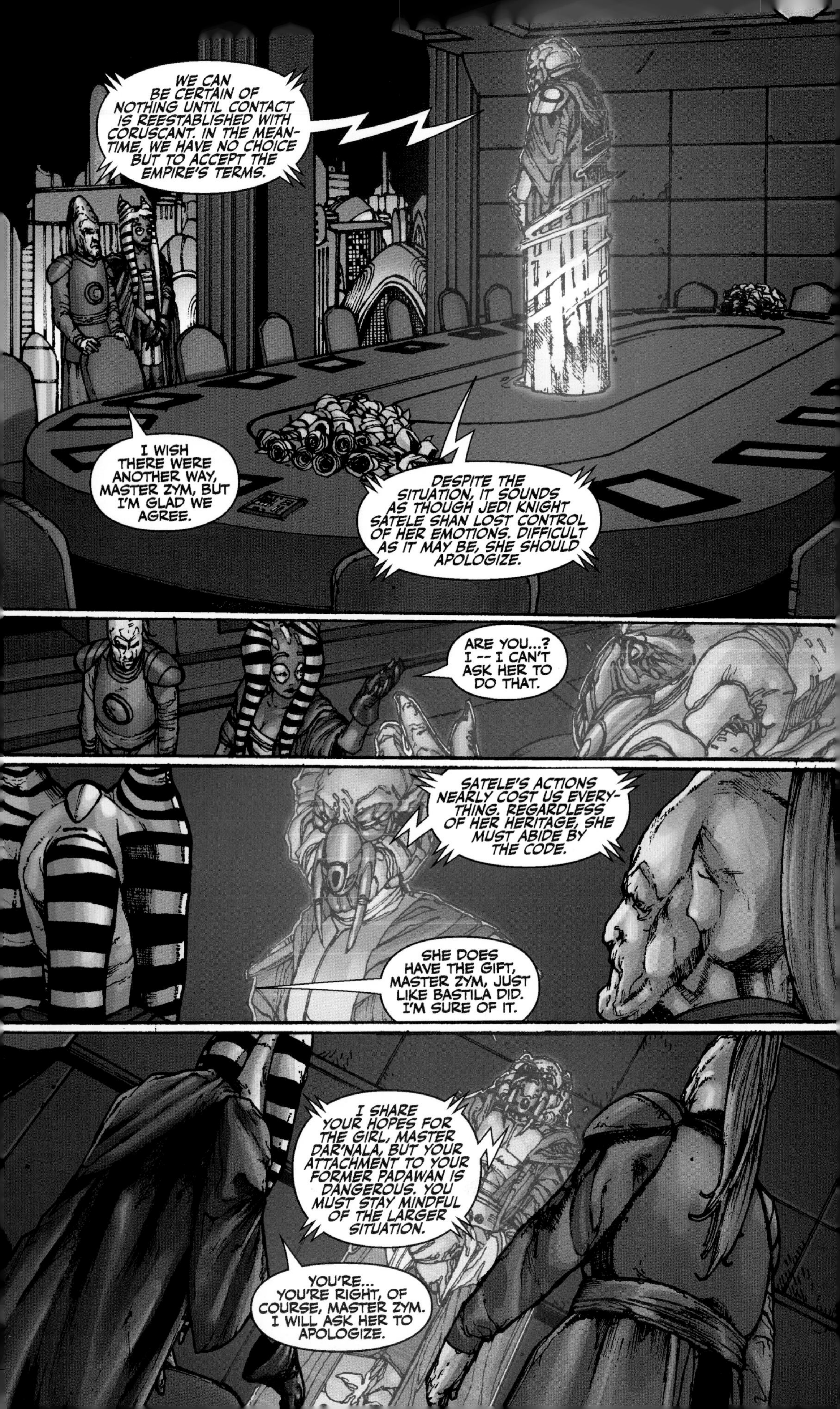
WE CAN BE CERTAIN OF NOTHING UNTIL CONTACT IS REESTABLISHED WITH CORUSCANT. IN THE MEAN-TIME, WE HAVE NO CHOICE BUT TO ACCEPT THE EMPIRE'S TERMS.
I WISH THERE WERE ANOTHER WAY, MASTER ZYM, BUT I'M GLAD WE AGREE.
DESPITE THE SITUATION, IT SOUNDS AS THOUGH JEDI KNIGHT SATELE SHAN LOST CONTROL OF HER EMOTIONS. DIFFICULT AS IT MAY BE, SHE SHOULD APOLOGIZE.
ARE YOU...? I -- I CAN'T ASK HER TO DO THAT.
SATELE'S ACTIONS NEARLY COST US EVERY-THING. REGARDLESS OF HER HERITAGE, SHE MUST ABIDE BY THE CODE.
SHE DOES HAVE THE GIFT, MASTER ZYM, JUST LIKE BASTILA DID. I'M SURE OF IT.
I SHARE YOUR HOPES FOR THE GIRL, MASTER DAR'NALA, BUT YOUR ATTACHMENT TO YOUR FORMER PADAWAN IS DANGEROUS. YOU MUST STAY MINDFUL OF THE LARGER SITUATION.
YOU'RE... YOU'RE RIGHT, OF COURSE, MASTER ZYM. I WILL ASK HER TO APOLOGIZE.

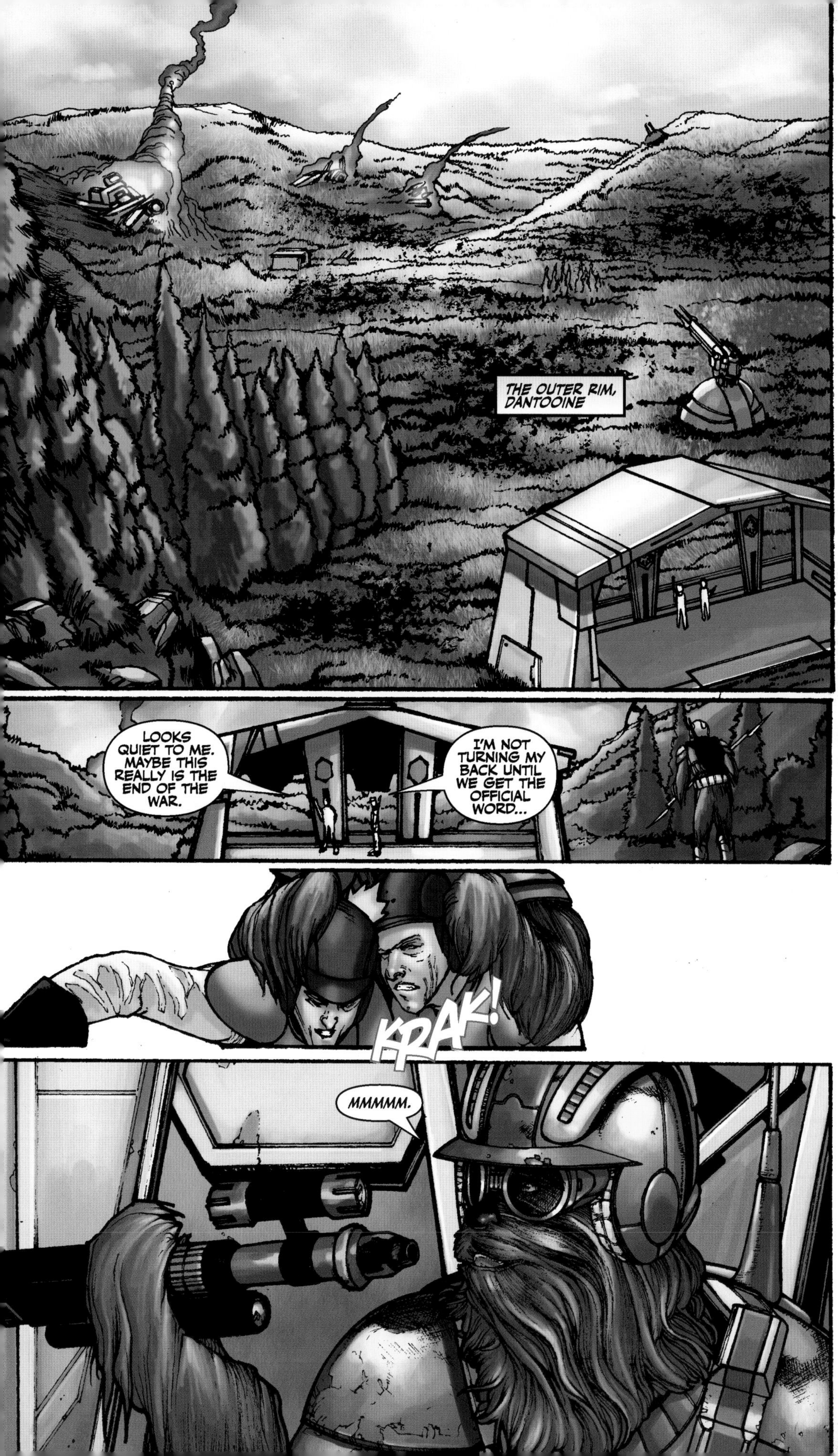
THE OUTER RIM, DANTOOINE
LOOKS QUIET TO ME. MAYBE THIS REALLY IS THE END OF THE WAR.
I'M NOT TURNING MY BACK UNTIL WE GET THE OFFICIAL WORD...
KRAK!
MMMMM.

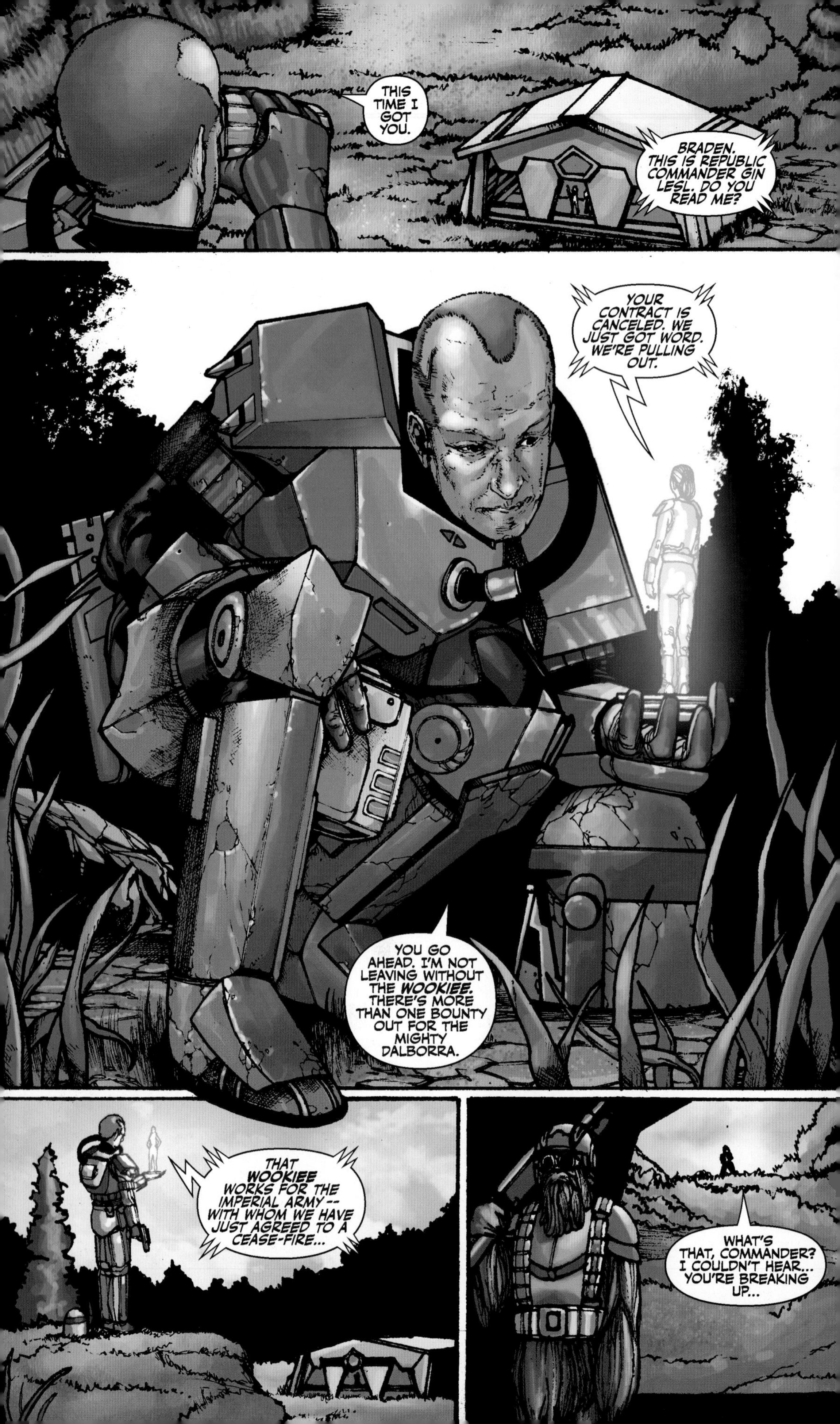
THIS TIME I GOT YOU.
BRADEN. THIS IS REPUBLIC COMMANDER GIN LESL. DO YOU READ ME?
YOUR CONTRACT IS CANCELED. WE JUST GOT WORD. WE'RE PULLING OUT.
YOU GO AHEAD. I'M NOT LEAVING WITHOUT THE WOOKIEE. THERE'S MORE THAN ONE BOUNTY OUT FOR THE MIGHTY DALBORRA.
THAT WOOKIEE WORKS FOR THE IMPERIAL ARMY-- WITH WHOM WE HAVE JUST AGREED TO A CEASE-FIRE...
WHAT'S THAT, COMMANDER? I COULDN'T HEAR... YOU'RE BREAKING UP...

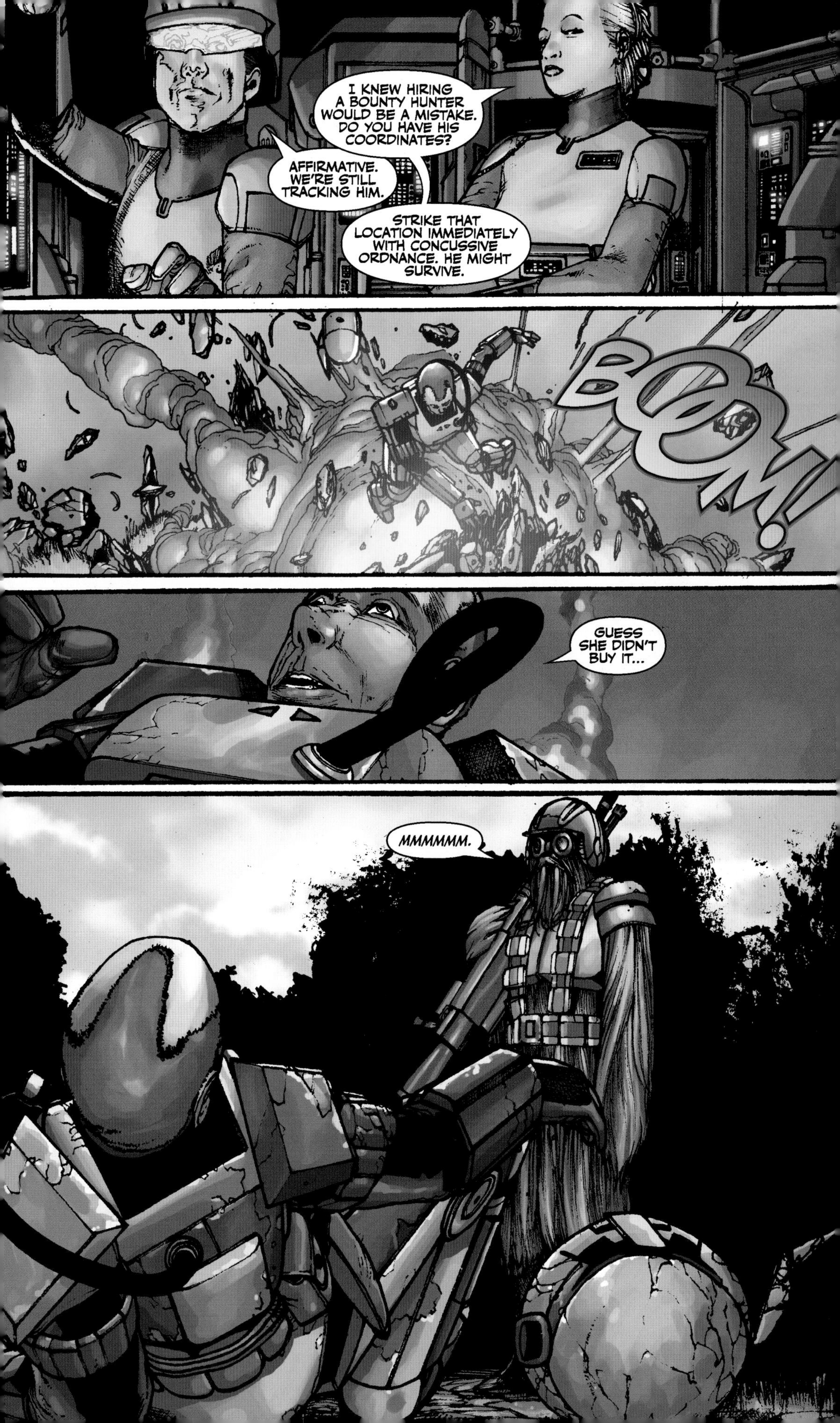
I KNEW HIRING A BOUNTY HUNTER WOULD BE A MISTAKE. DO YOU HAVE HIS COORDINATES?
AFFIRMATIVE. WE'RE STILL TRACKING HIM.
STRIKE THAT LOCATION IMMEDIATELY WITH CONCUSSIVE ORDNANCE. HE MIGHT SURVIVE.
BOOM!
GUESS SHE DIDN'T BUY IT...
MMMMMM.

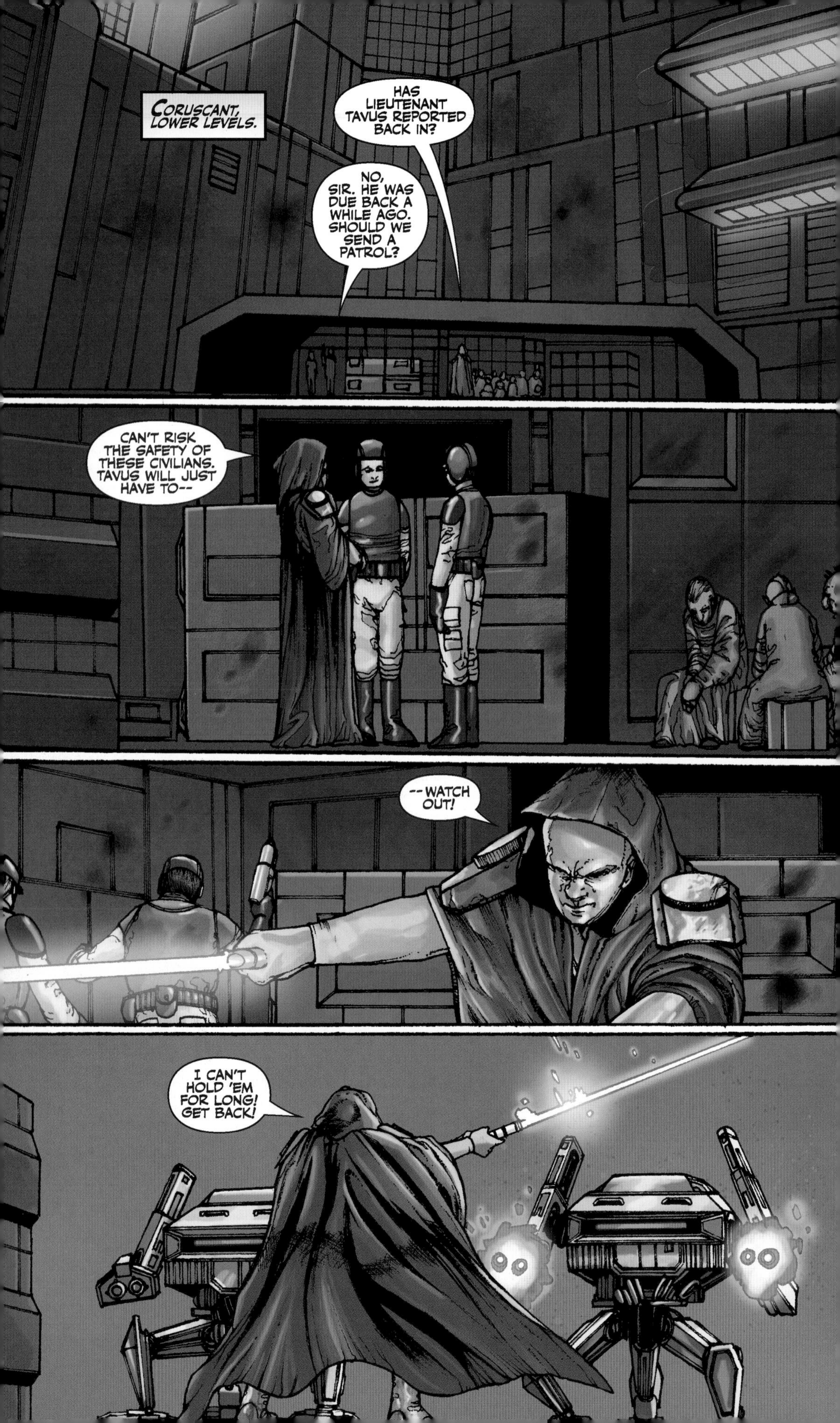
Coruscant, lower levels.
Has Lieutenant Tavus reported back in?
No, sir. He was due back a while ago. Should we send a patrol?
Can't risk the safety of these civilians. Tavus will just have to--
--watch out!
I can't hold 'em for long! Get back!

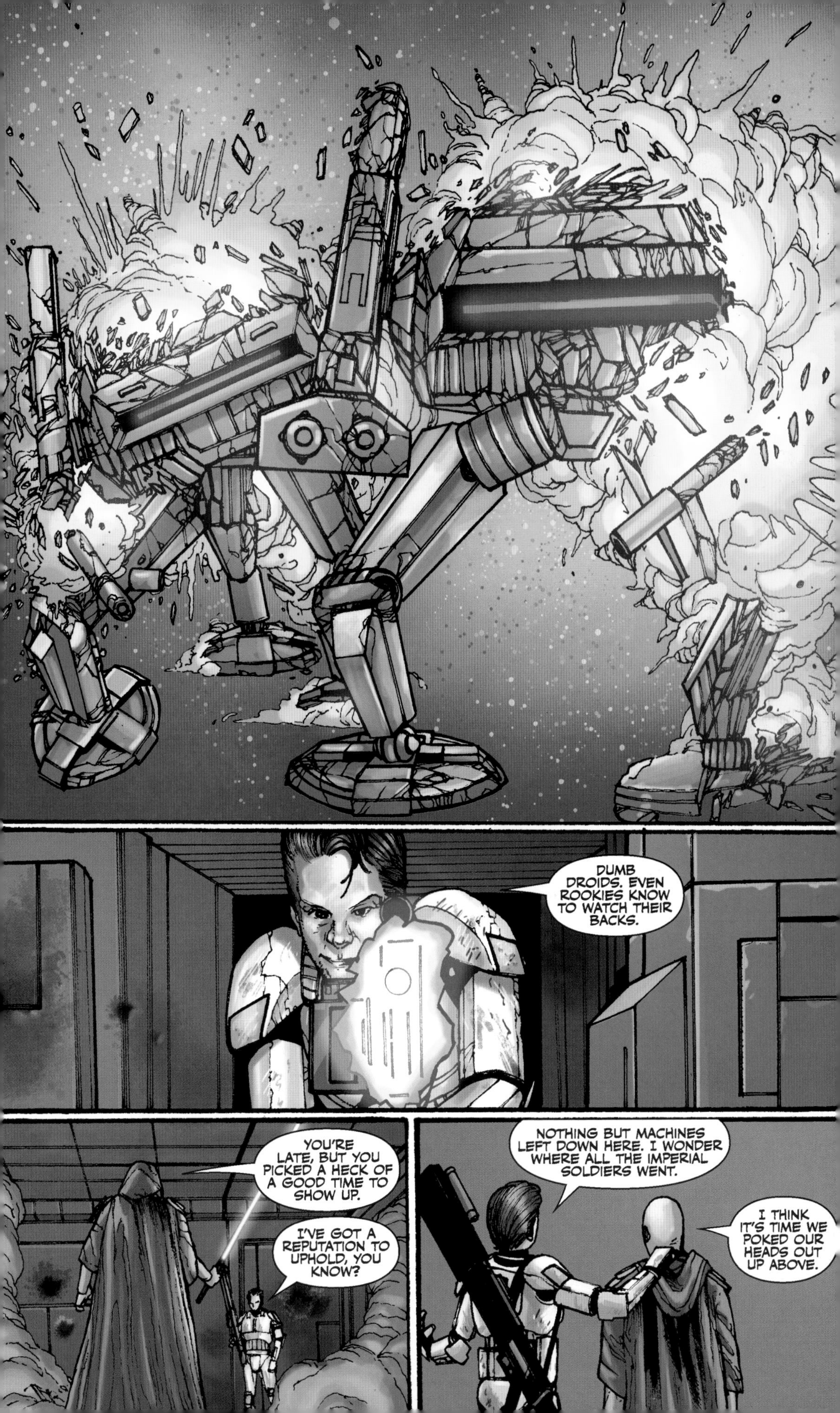
DUMB DROIDS. EVEN ROOKIES KNOW TO WATCH THEIR BACKS.
YOU'RE LATE, BUT YOU PICKED A HECK OF A GOOD TIME TO SHOW UP.
I'VE GOT A REPUTATION TO UPHOLD, YOU KNOW?
NOTHING BUT MACHINES LEFT DOWN HERE. I WONDER WHERE ALL THE IMPERIAL SOLDIERS WENT.
I THINK IT'S TIME WE POKED OUR HEADS OUT UP ABOVE.

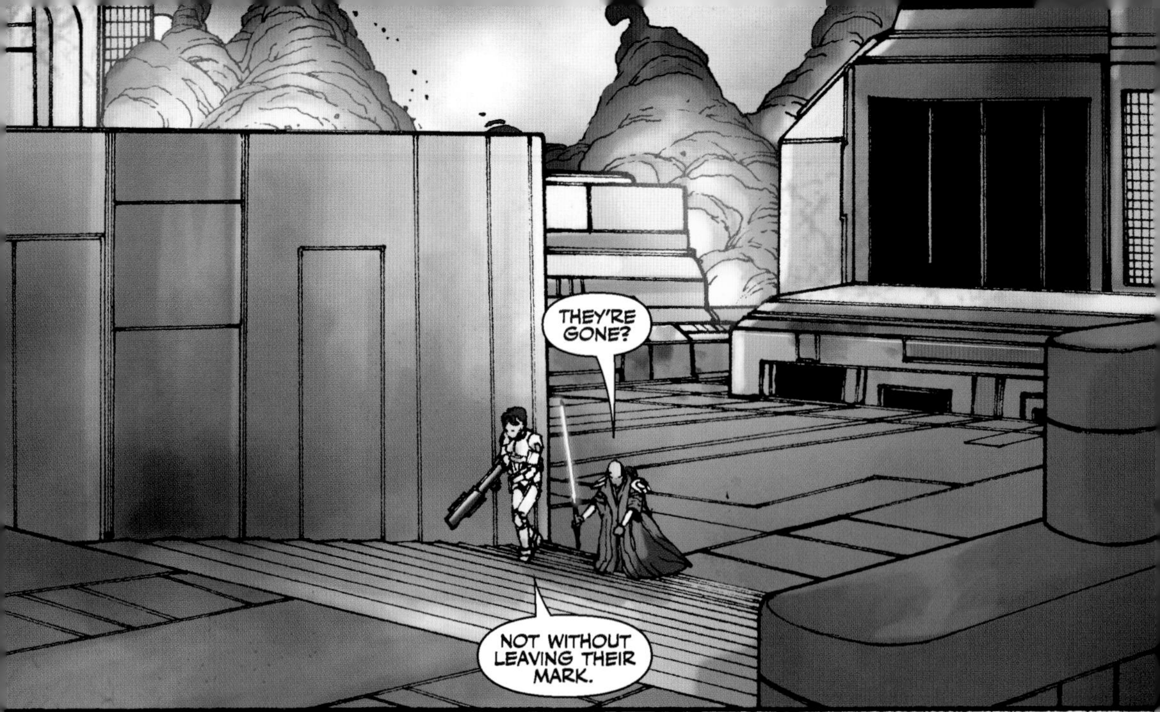
THEY'RE GONE?
NOT WITHOUT LEAVING THEIR MARK.

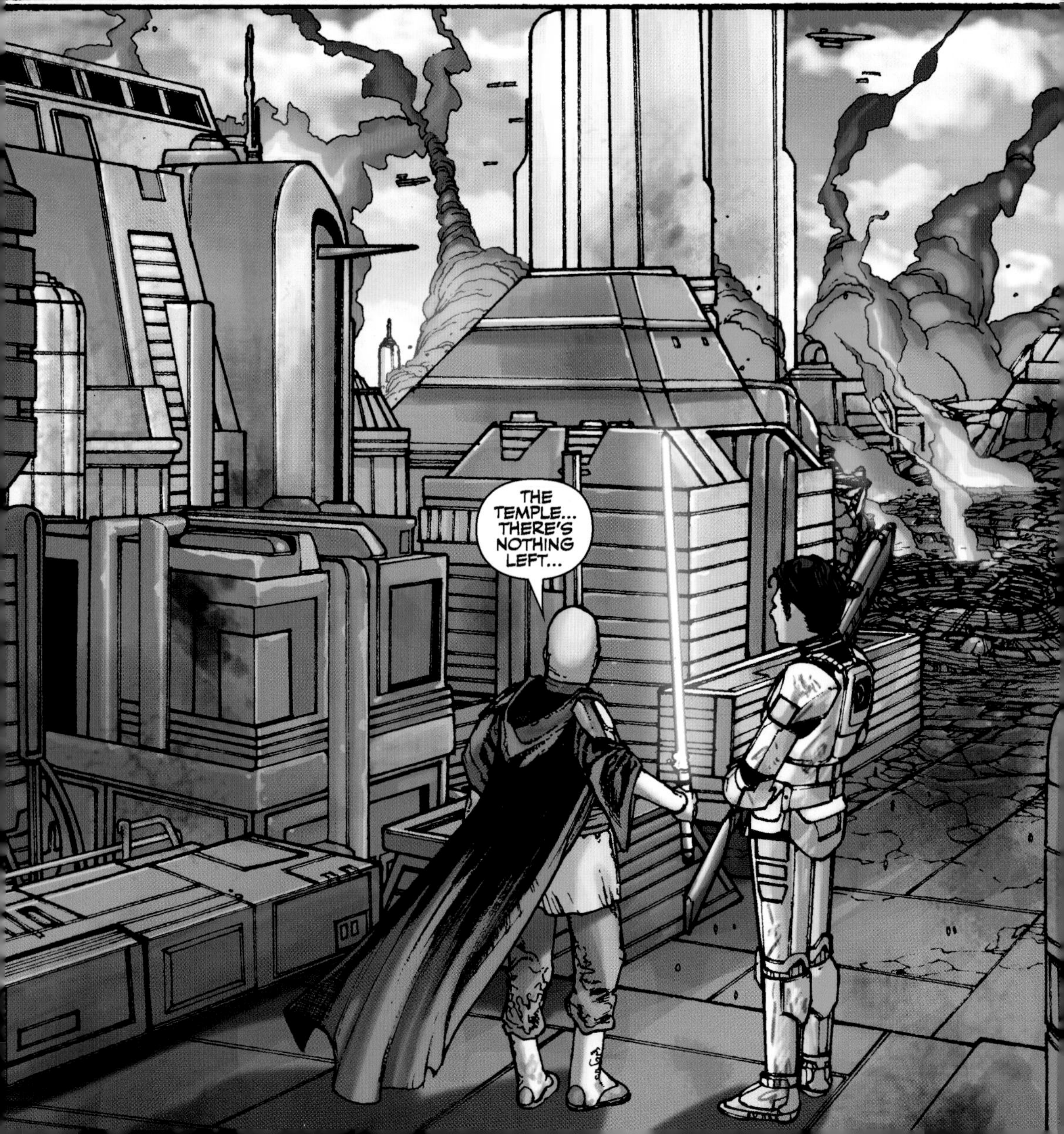
THE TEMPLE... THERE'S NOTHING LEFT...

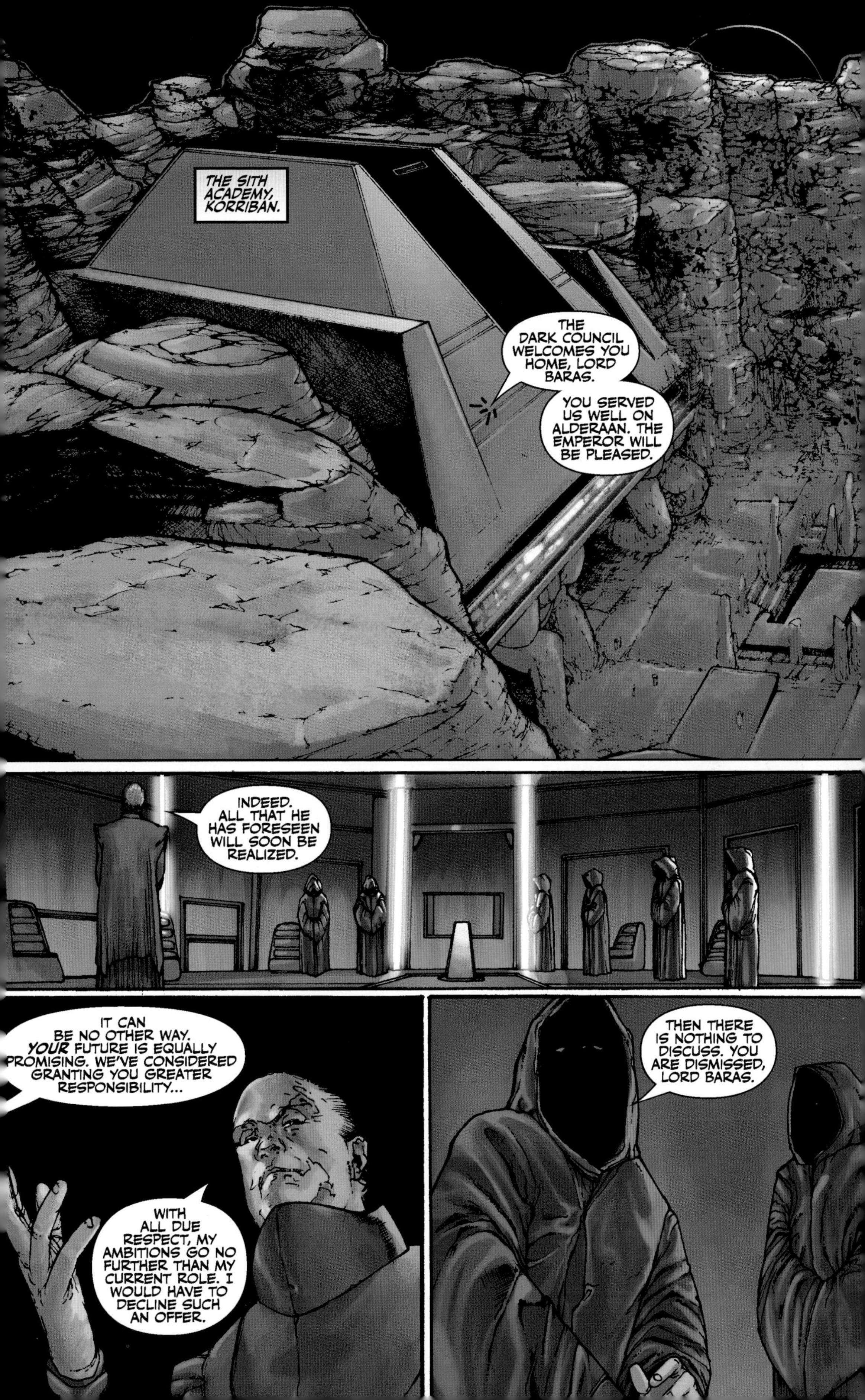
THE SITH ACADEMY, KORRIBAN.
THE DARK COUNCIL WELCOMES YOU HOME, LORD BARAS.
YOU SERVED US WELL ON ALDERAAN. THE EMPEROR WILL BE PLEASED.
INDEED. ALL THAT HE HAS FORESEEN WILL SOON BE REALIZED.
IT CAN BE NO OTHER WAY. YOUR FUTURE IS EQUALLY PROMISING. WE'VE CONSIDERED GRANTING YOU GREATER RESPONSIBILITY...
WITH ALL DUE RESPECT, MY AMBITIONS GO NO FURTHER THAN MY CURRENT ROLE. I WOULD HAVE TO DECLINE SUCH AN OFFER.
THEN THERE IS NOTHING TO DISCUSS. YOU ARE DISMISSED, LORD BARAS.

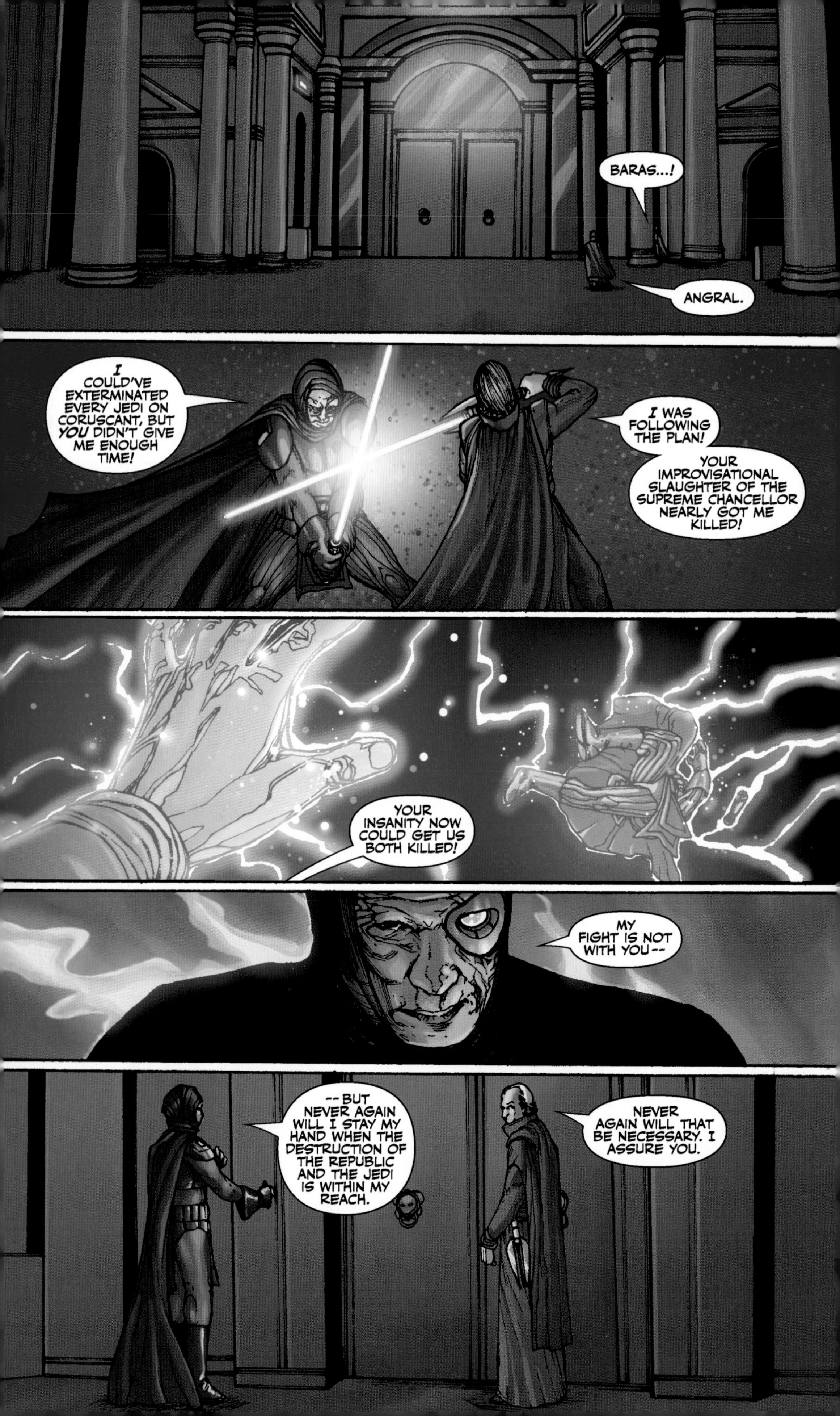
BARAS...!
ANGRAL.
I COULD'VE EXTERMINATED EVERY JEDI ON CORUSCANT, BUT YOU DIDN'T GIVE ME ENOUGH TIME!
I WAS FOLLOWING THE PLAN!
YOUR IMPROVISATIONAL SLAUGHTER OF THE SUPREME CHANCELLOR NEARLY GOT ME KILLED!
YOUR INSANITY NOW COULD GET US BOTH KILLED!
MY FIGHT IS NOT WITH YOU--
--BUT NEVER AGAIN WILL I STAY MY HAND WHEN THE DESTRUCTION OF THE REPUBLIC AND THE JEDI IS WITHIN MY REACH.
NEVER AGAIN WILL THAT BE NECESSARY. I ASSURE YOU.

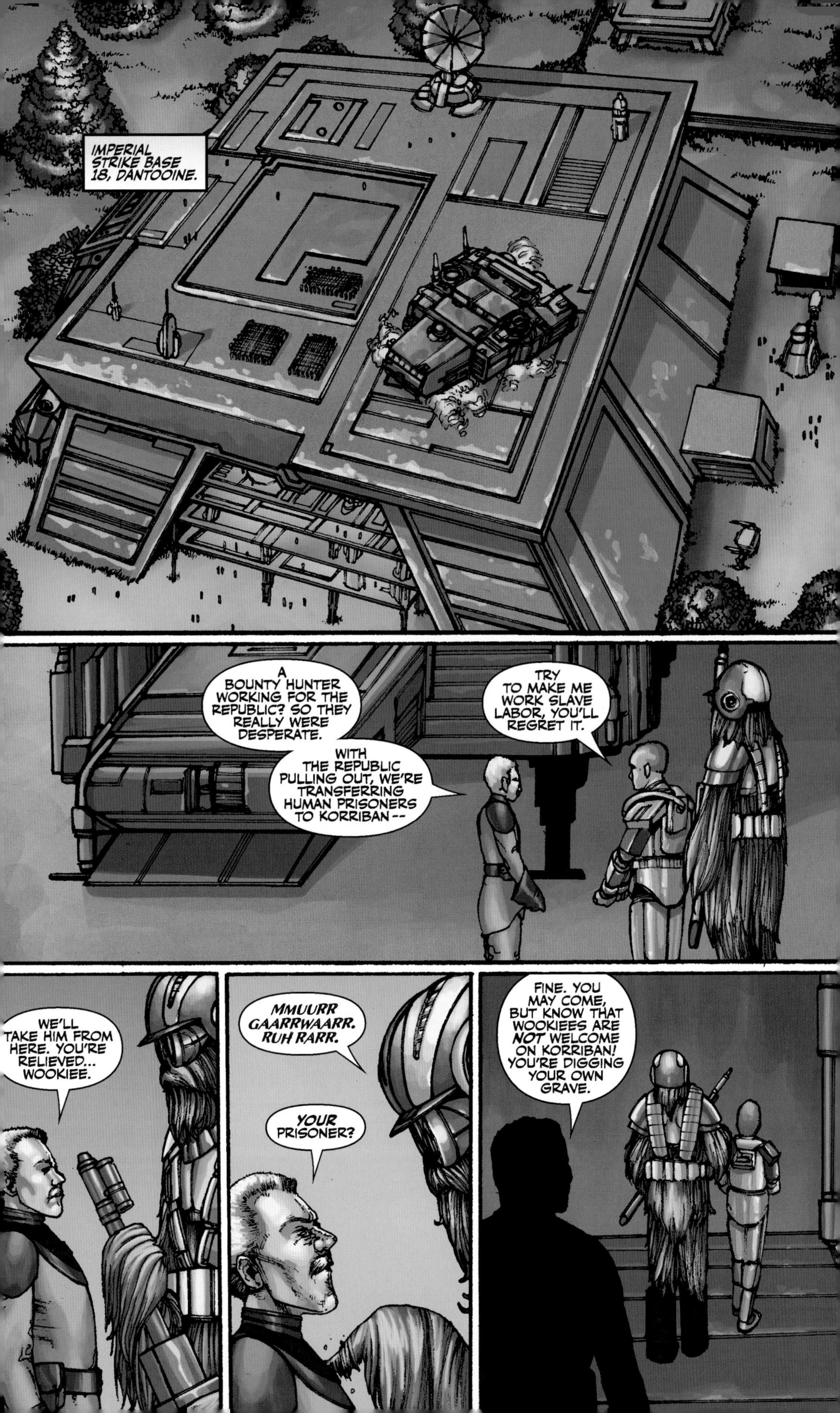
IMPERIAL STRIKE BASE 18, DANTOOINE.
A BOUNTY HUNTER WORKING FOR THE REPUBLIC? SO THEY REALLY WERE DESPERATE.
WITH THE REPUBLIC PULLING OUT, WE'RE TRANSFERRING HUMAN PRISONERS TO KORRIBAN--
TRY TO MAKE ME WORK SLAVE LABOR, YOU'LL REGRET IT.
WE'LL TAKE HIM FROM HERE. YOU'RE RELIEVED... WOOKIEE.
MMUURR GAARRWAARR. RUH RARR.
YOUR PRISONER?
FINE. YOU MAY COME, BUT KNOW THAT WOOKIEES ARE NOT WELCOME ON KORRIBAN! YOU'RE DIGGING YOUR OWN GRAVE.

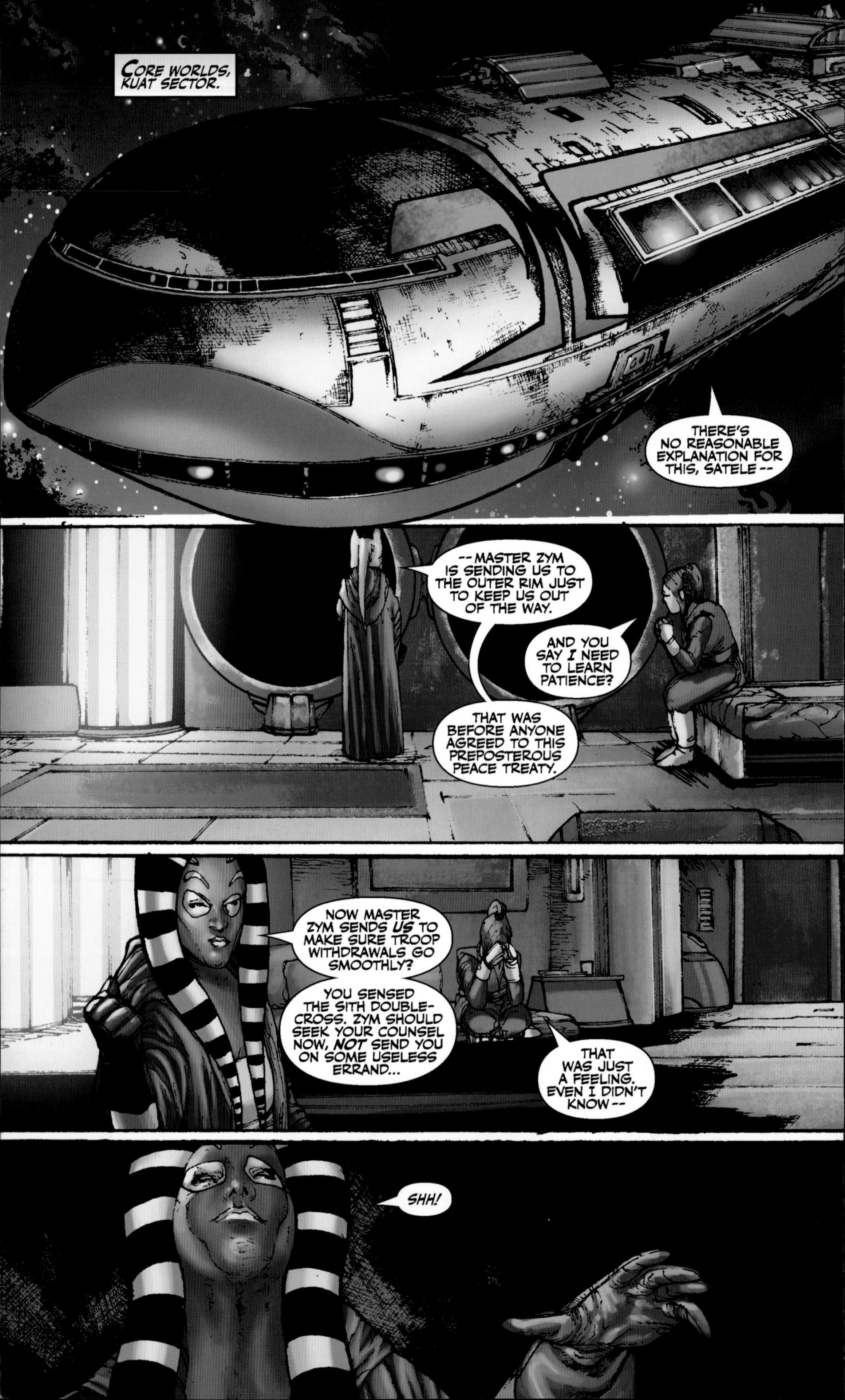
CORE WORLDS, KUAT SECTOR.
THERE'S NO REASONABLE EXPLANATION FOR THIS, SATELE--
--MASTER ZYM IS SENDING US TO THE OUTER RIM JUST TO KEEP US OUT OF THE WAY.
AND YOU SAY *I* NEED TO LEARN PATIENCE?
THAT WAS BEFORE ANYONE AGREED TO THIS PREPOSTEROUS PEACE TREATY.
NOW MASTER ZYM SENDS *US* TO MAKE SURE TROOP WITHDRAWALS GO SMOOTHLY?
YOU SENSED THE SITH DOUBLE-CROSS. ZYM SHOULD SEEK YOUR COUNSEL NOW, *NOT* SEND YOU ON SOME USELESS ERRAND...
THAT WAS JUST A FEELING. EVEN I DIDN'T KNOW--
SHH!

YOU'RE SPYING ON US?! GIVE ME ONE REASON NOT TO MELT YOUR MEMORY CORE!

THE PRIMARY REASON IS THAT YOU SIGNED A PEACE AGREEMENT WITH THE EMPIRE. HARMING ME WOULD BE A VIOLATION OF THE TERMS.

I WOULD ALSO REMIND YOU THAT MY ASSIGNMENT HERE IS TO MONITOR REPUBLIC AND JEDI ACTIVITIES AND ENSURE COMPLIANCE WITH THE TREATY.

IT *IS* HIS JOB TO WATCH US, MASTER.

THEN WE'LL SPEAK LATER, SATELE... WHEN WE CAN DO SO MORE PRIVATELY.

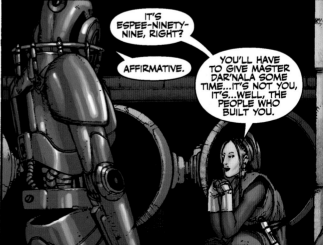

IT'S ESPEE-NINETY-NINE, RIGHT?

AFFIRMATIVE.

YOU'LL HAVE TO GIVE MASTER DAR'NALA SOME TIME...IT'S NOT YOU, IT'S...WELL, THE PEOPLE WHO BUILT YOU.

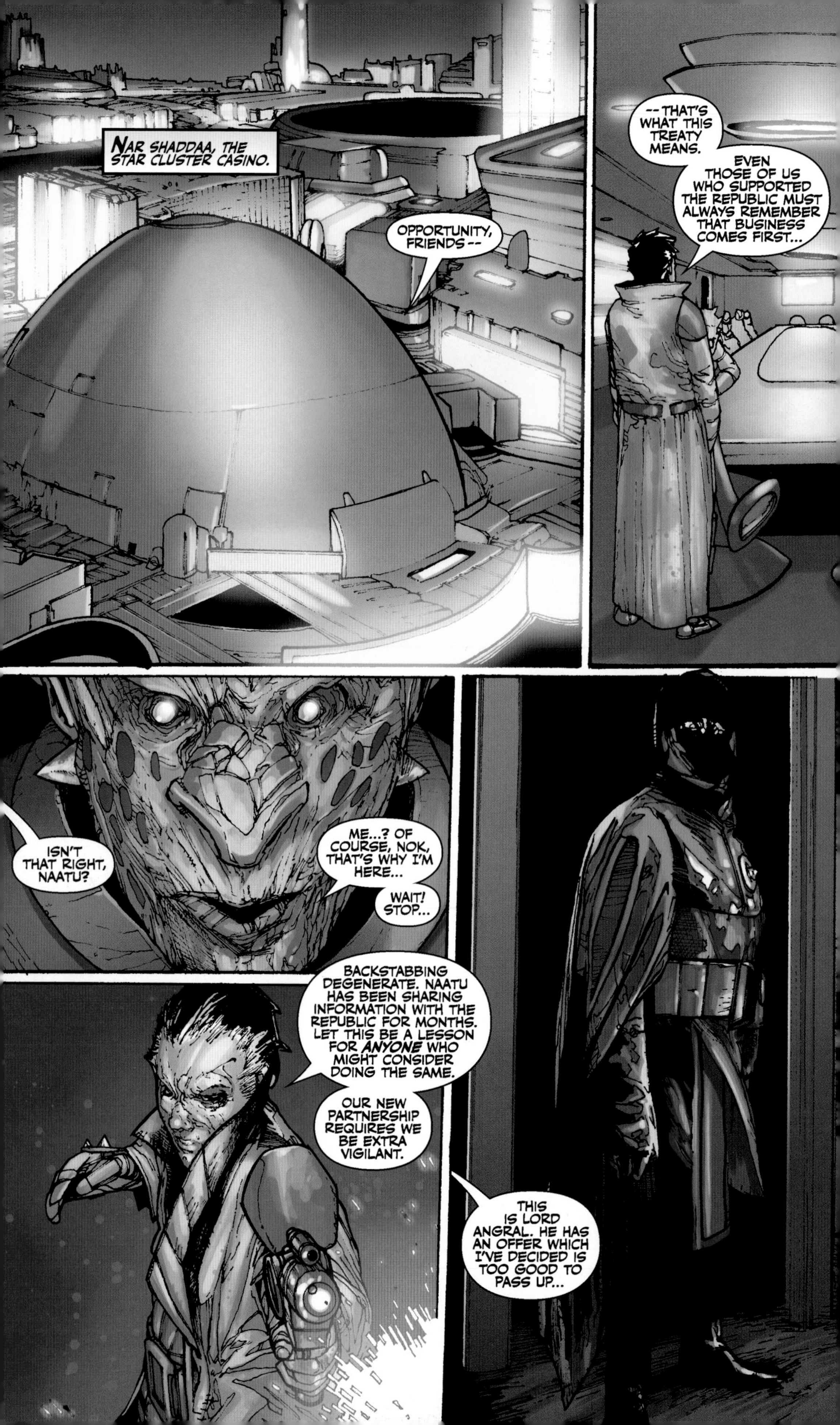
NAR SHADDAA, THE STAR CLUSTER CASINO.
OPPORTUNITY, FRIENDS --
-- THAT'S WHAT THIS TREATY MEANS.
EVEN THOSE OF US WHO SUPPORTED THE REPUBLIC MUST ALWAYS REMEMBER THAT BUSINESS COMES FIRST...
ISN'T THAT RIGHT, NAATU?
ME...? OF COURSE, NOK, THAT'S WHY I'M HERE...
WAIT! STOP...
BACKSTABBING DEGENERATE. NAATU HAS BEEN SHARING INFORMATION WITH THE REPUBLIC FOR MONTHS. LET THIS BE A LESSON FOR ANYONE WHO MIGHT CONSIDER DOING THE SAME.
OUR NEW PARTNERSHIP REQUIRES WE BE EXTRA VIGILANT.
THIS IS LORD ANGRAL. HE HAS AN OFFER WHICH I'VE DECIDED IS TOO GOOD TO PASS UP...

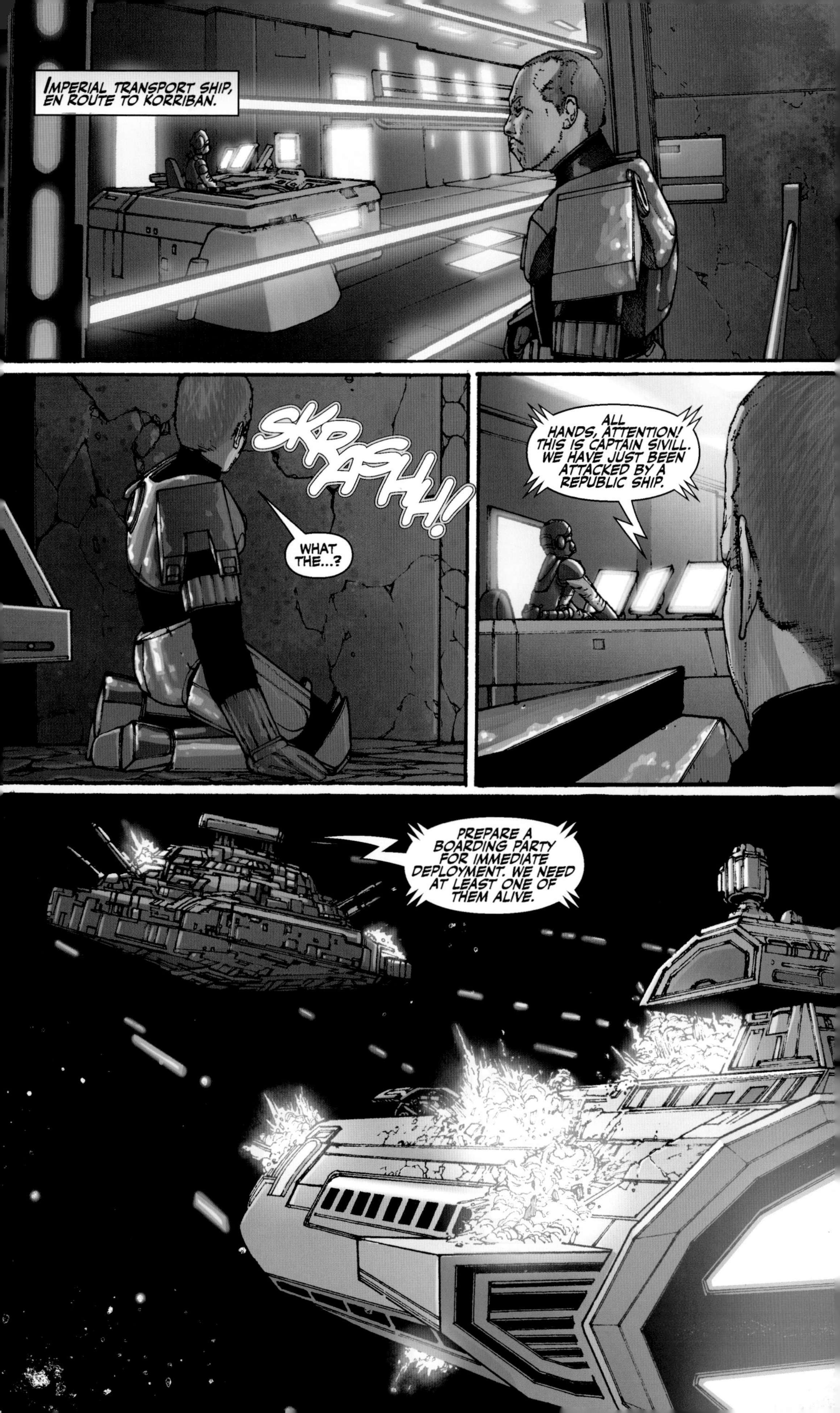
IMPERIAL TRANSPORT SHIP, EN ROUTE TO KORRIBAN.
SKRASHH!
WHAT THE...?
ALL HANDS, ATTENTION! THIS IS CAPTAIN SIVILL. WE HAVE JUST BEEN ATTACKED BY A REPUBLIC SHIP.
PREPARE A BOARDING PARTY FOR IMMEDIATE DEPLOYMENT. WE NEED AT LEAST ONE OF THEM ALIVE.

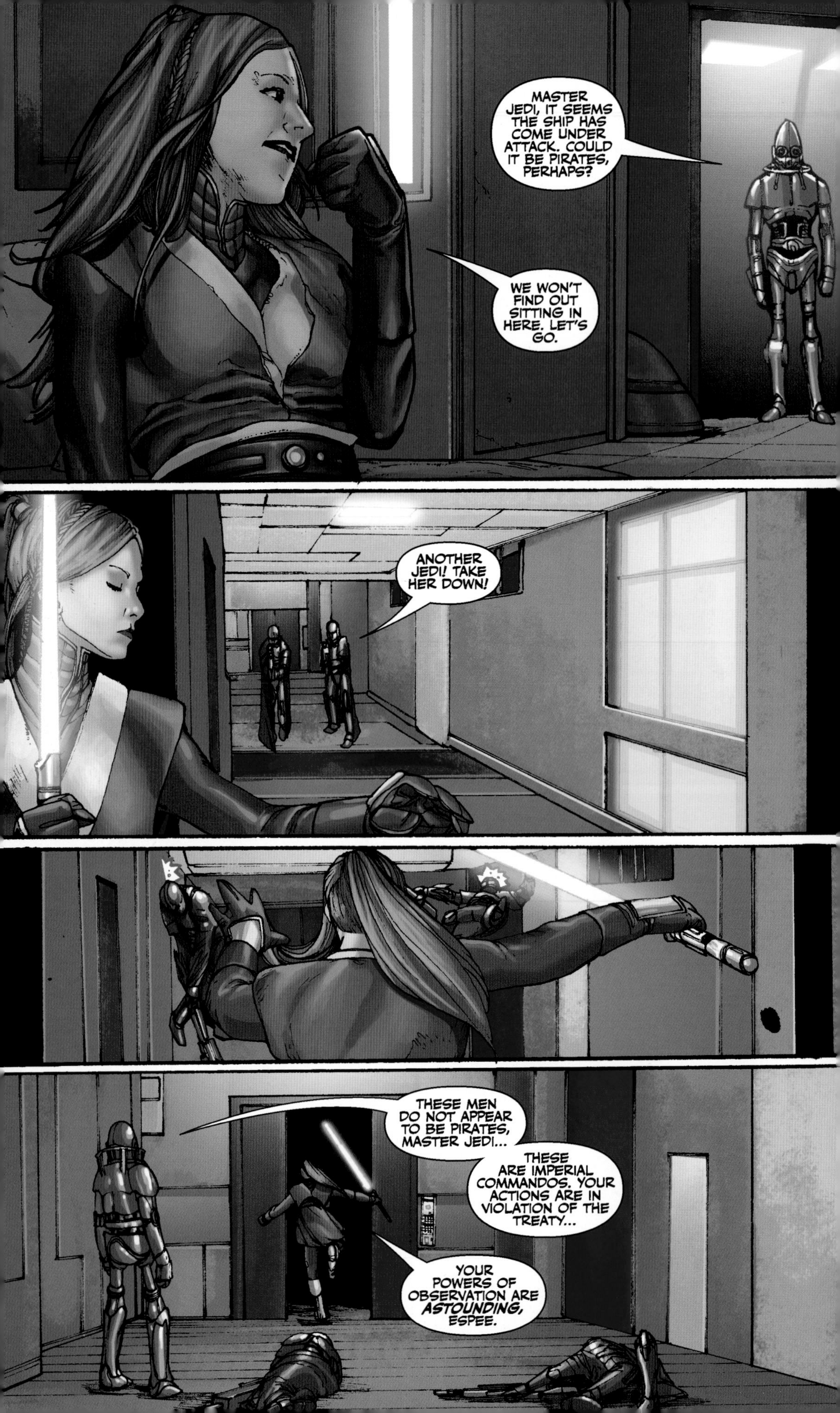
MASTER JEDI, IT SEEMS THE SHIP HAS COME UNDER ATTACK. COULD IT BE PIRATES, PERHAPS?
WE WON'T FIND OUT SITTING IN HERE. LET'S GO.
ANOTHER JEDI! TAKE HER DOWN!
THESE MEN DO NOT APPEAR TO BE PIRATES, MASTER JEDI...
THESE ARE IMPERIAL COMMANDOS. YOUR ACTIONS ARE IN VIOLATION OF THE TREATY...
YOUR POWERS OF OBSERVATION ARE *ASTOUNDING,* ESPEE.

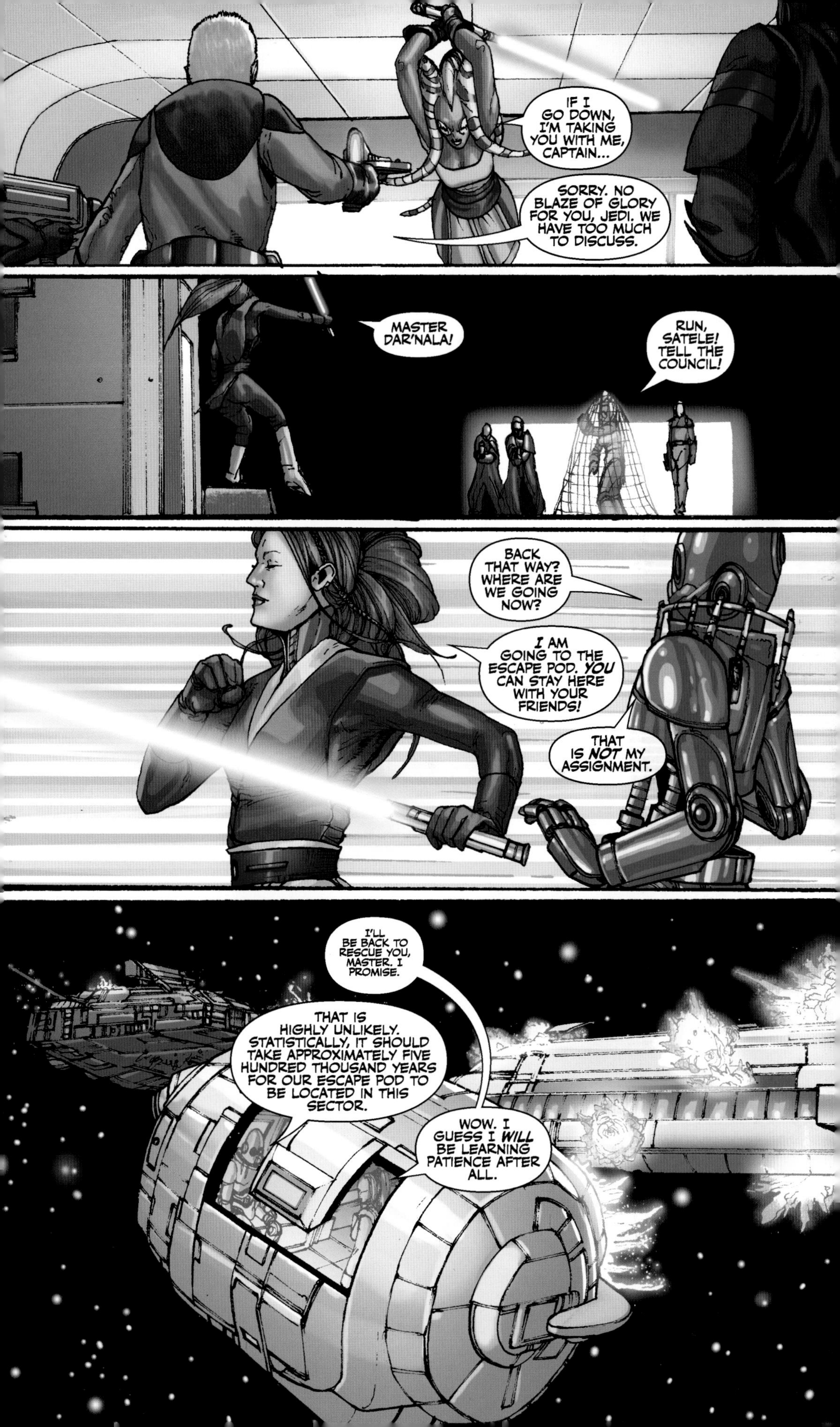
IF I GO DOWN, I'M TAKING YOU WITH ME, CAPTAIN...
SORRY. NO BLAZE OF GLORY FOR YOU, JEDI. WE HAVE TOO MUCH TO DISCUSS.
MASTER DAR'NALA!
RUN, SATELE! TELL THE COUNCIL!
BACK THAT WAY? WHERE ARE WE GOING NOW?
I AM GOING TO THE ESCAPE POD. YOU CAN STAY HERE WITH YOUR FRIENDS!
THAT IS NOT MY ASSIGNMENT.
I'LL BE BACK TO RESCUE YOU, MASTER. I PROMISE.
THAT IS HIGHLY UNLIKELY. STATISTICALLY, IT SHOULD TAKE APPROXIMATELY FIVE HUNDRED THOUSAND YEARS FOR OUR ESCAPE POD TO BE LOCATED IN THIS SECTOR.
WOW. I GUESS I WILL BE LEARNING PATIENCE AFTER ALL.

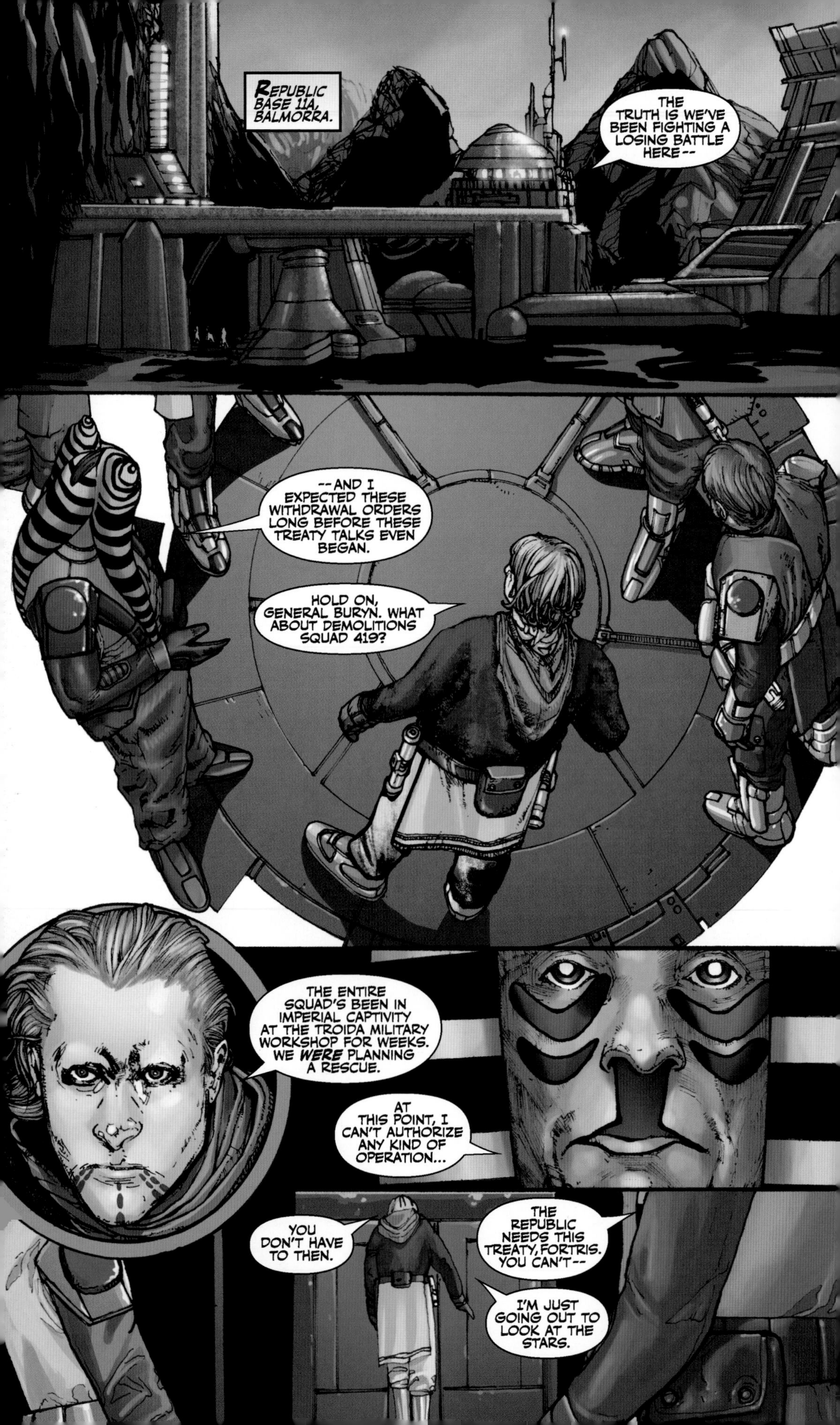
REPUBLIC BASE 11A, BALMORRA.
THE TRUTH IS WE'VE BEEN FIGHTING A LOSING BATTLE HERE--
--AND I EXPECTED THESE WITHDRAWAL ORDERS LONG BEFORE THESE TREATY TALKS EVEN BEGAN.
HOLD ON, GENERAL BURYN. WHAT ABOUT DEMOLITIONS SQUAD 419?
THE ENTIRE SQUAD'S BEEN IN IMPERIAL CAPTIVITY AT THE TROIDA MILITARY WORKSHOP FOR WEEKS. WE *WERE* PLANNING A RESCUE.
AT THIS POINT, I CAN'T AUTHORIZE ANY KIND OF OPERATION...
YOU DON'T HAVE TO THEN.
THE REPUBLIC NEEDS THIS TREATY, FORTRIS. YOU CAN'T--
I'M JUST GOING OUT TO LOOK AT THE STARS.

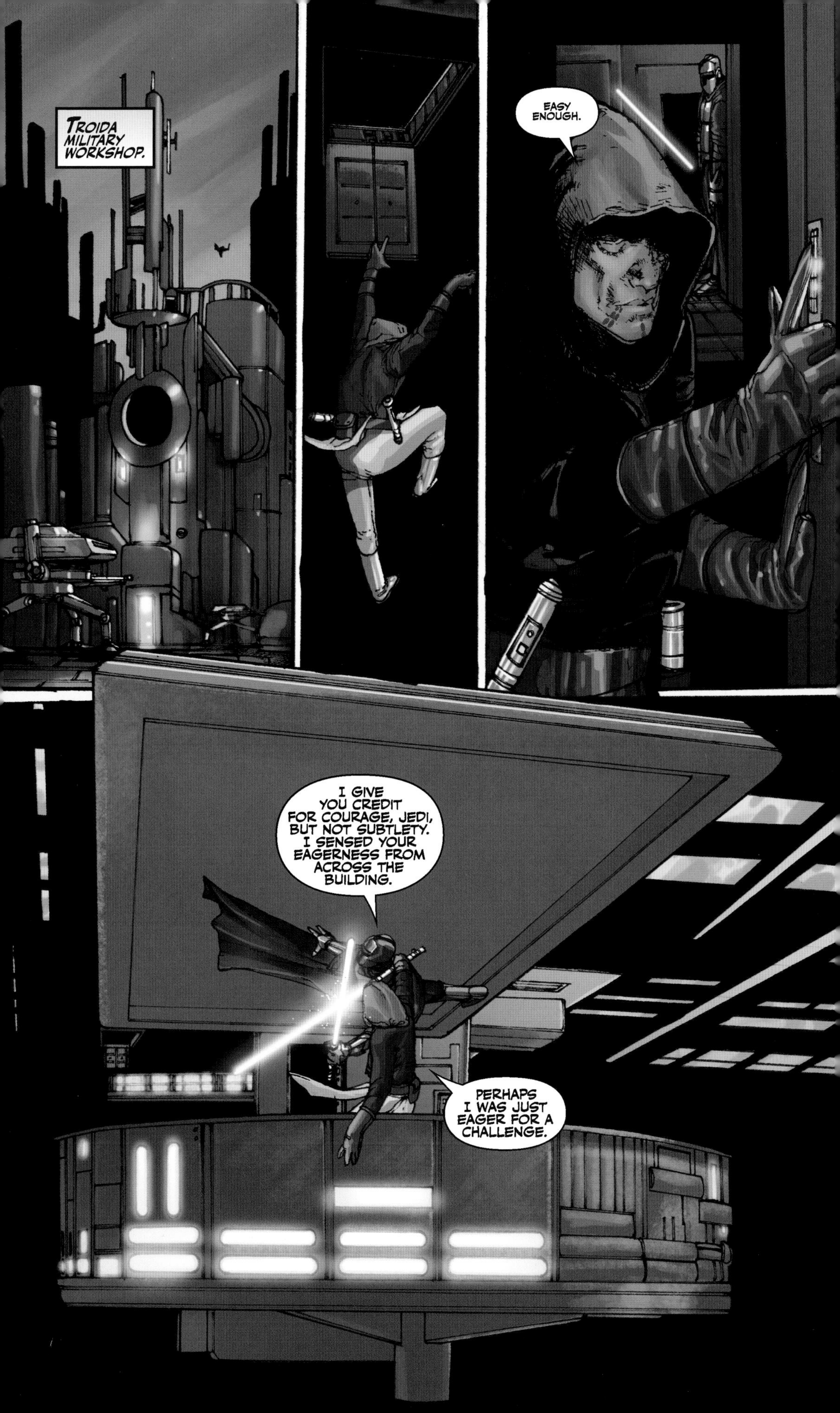
TROIDA MILITARY WORKSHOP.
EASY ENOUGH.
I GIVE YOU CREDIT FOR COURAGE, JEDI, BUT NOT SUBTLETY. I SENSED YOUR EAGERNESS FROM ACROSS THE BUILDING.
PERHAPS I WAS JUST EAGER FOR A CHALLENGE.

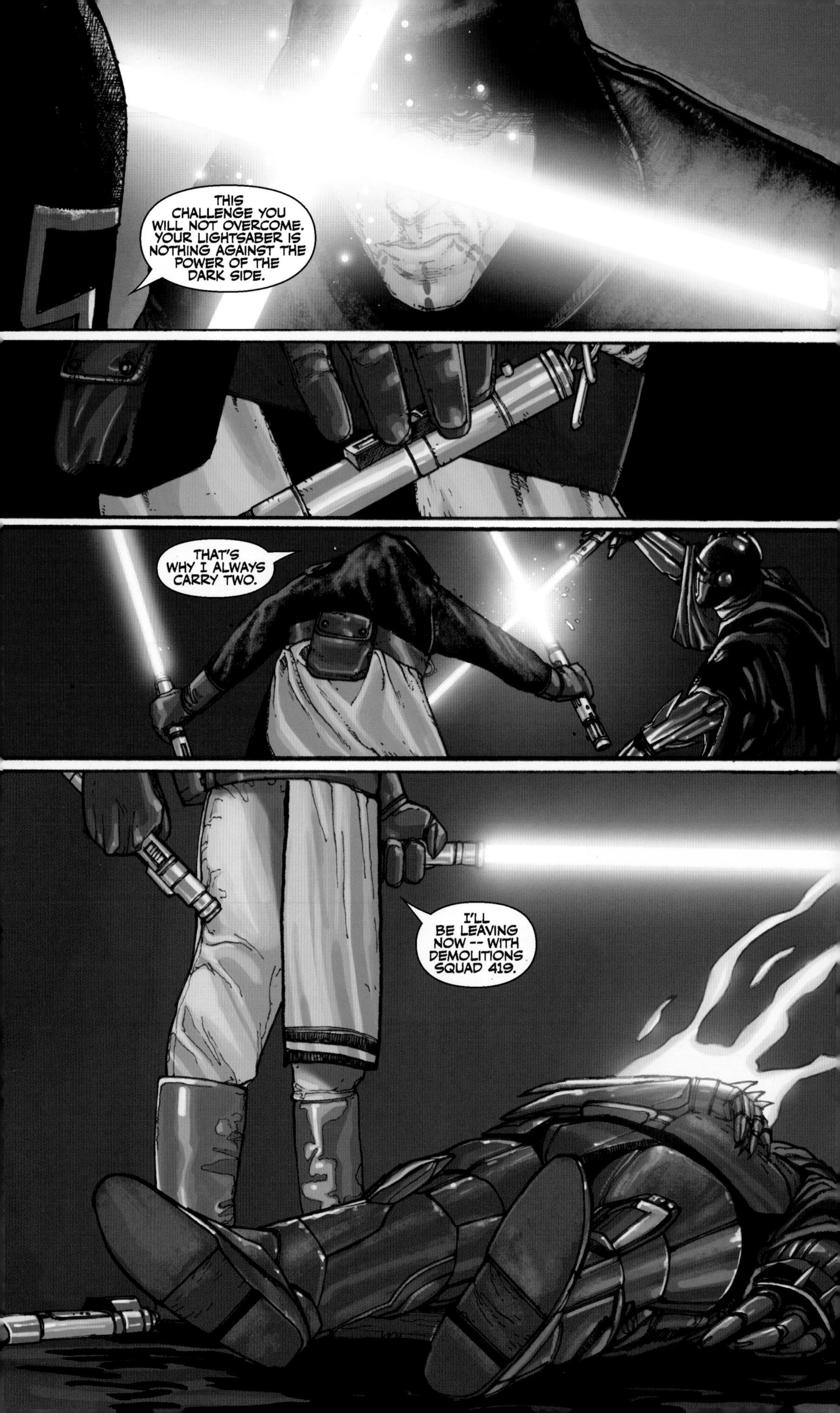
THIS CHALLENGE YOU WILL NOT OVERCOME. YOUR LIGHTSABER IS NOTHING AGAINST THE POWER OF THE DARK SIDE.
THAT'S WHY I ALWAYS CARRY TWO.
I'LL BE LEAVING NOW -- WITH DEMOLITIONS SQUAD 419.

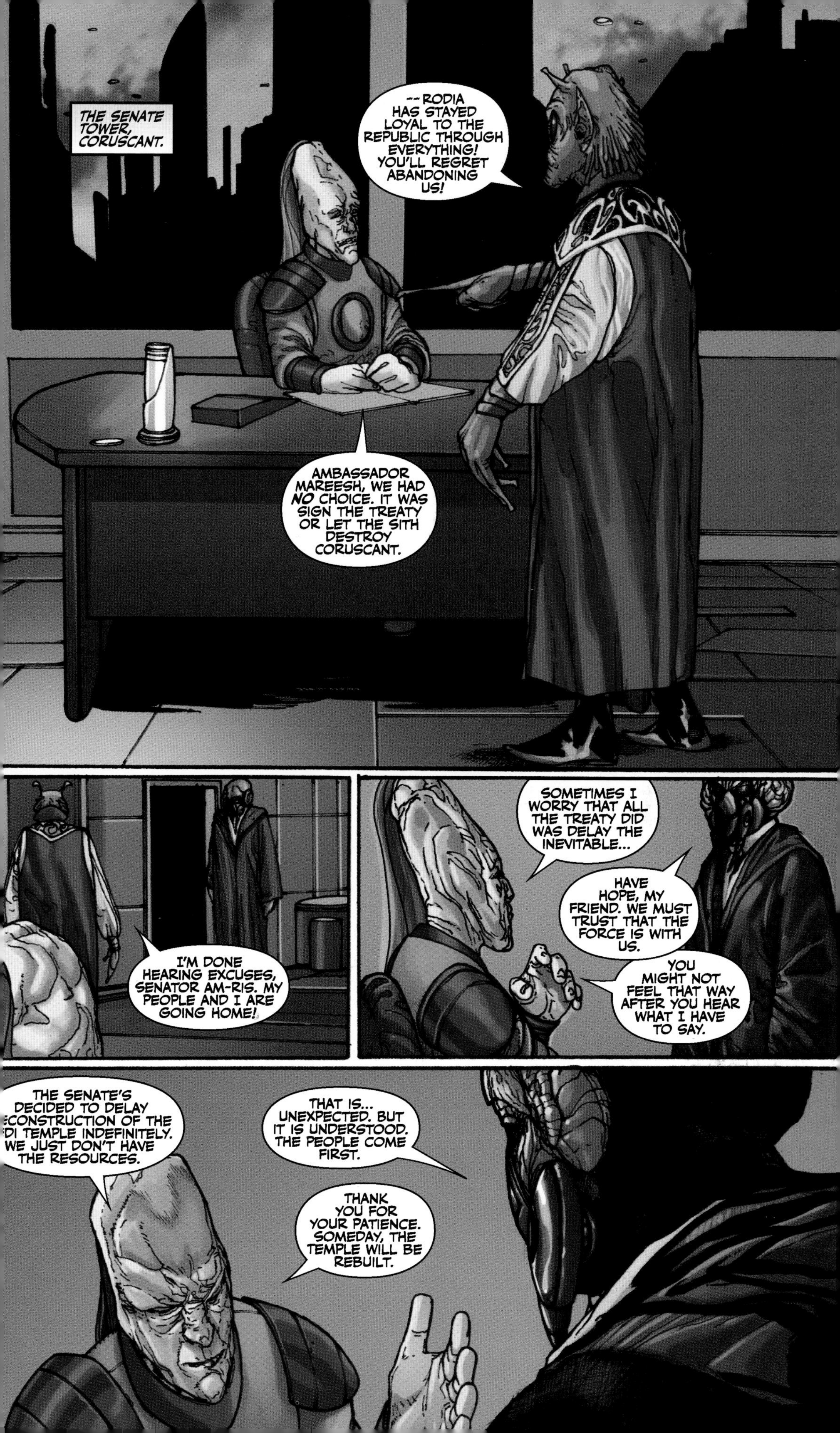
THE SENATE TOWER, CORUSCANT.
--RODIA HAS STAYED LOYAL TO THE REPUBLIC THROUGH EVERYTHING! YOU'LL REGRET ABANDONING US!
AMBASSADOR MAREESH, WE HAD NO CHOICE. IT WAS SIGN THE TREATY OR LET THE SITH DESTROY CORUSCANT.
I'M DONE HEARING EXCUSES, SENATOR AM-RIS. MY PEOPLE AND I ARE GOING HOME!
SOMETIMES I WORRY THAT ALL THE TREATY DID WAS DELAY THE INEVITABLE...
HAVE HOPE, MY FRIEND. WE MUST TRUST THAT THE FORCE IS WITH US.
YOU MIGHT NOT FEEL THAT WAY AFTER YOU HEAR WHAT I HAVE TO SAY.
THE SENATE'S DECIDED TO DELAY ECONSTRUCTION OF THE DI TEMPLE INDEFINITELY. WE JUST DON'T HAVE THE RESOURCES.
THAT IS... UNEXPECTED. BUT IT IS UNDERSTOOD. THE PEOPLE COME FIRST.
THANK YOU FOR YOUR PATIENCE. SOMEDAY, THE TEMPLE WILL BE REBUILT.

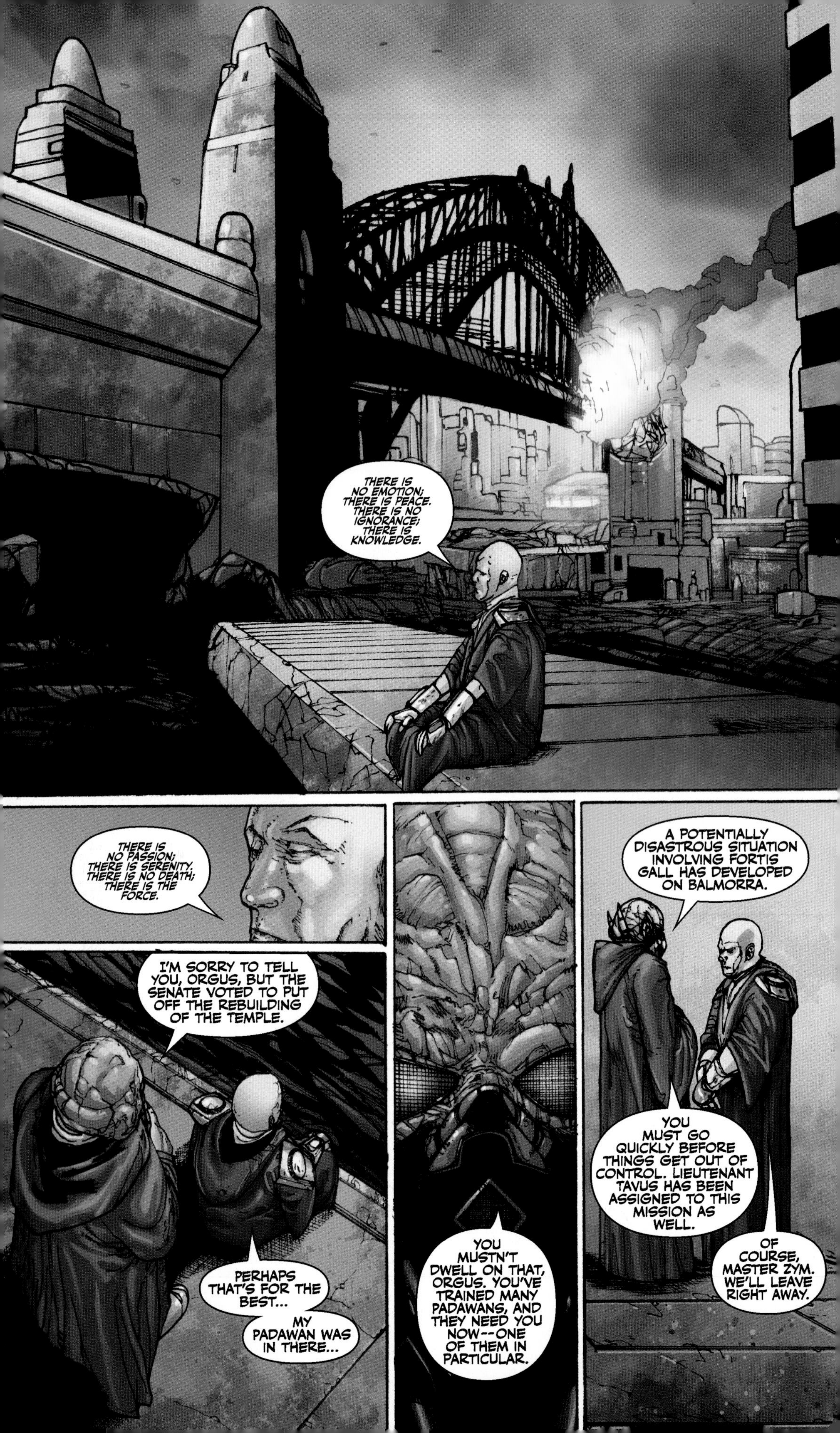
THERE IS NO EMOTION; THERE IS PEACE. THERE IS NO IGNORANCE; THERE IS KNOWLEDGE.
THERE IS NO PASSION; THERE IS SERENITY. THERE IS NO DEATH; THERE IS THE FORCE.
I'M SORRY TO TELL YOU, ORGUS, BUT THE SENATE VOTED TO PUT OFF THE REBUILDING OF THE TEMPLE.
PERHAPS THAT'S FOR THE BEST...
MY PADAWAN WAS IN THERE...
YOU MUSTN'T DWELL ON THAT, ORGUS. YOU'VE TRAINED MANY PADAWANS, AND THEY NEED YOU NOW--ONE OF THEM IN PARTICULAR.
A POTENTIALLY DISASTROUS SITUATION INVOLVING FORTIS GALL HAS DEVELOPED ON BALMORRA.
YOU MUST GO QUICKLY BEFORE THINGS GET OUT OF CONTROL. LIEUTENANT TAVUS HAS BEEN ASSIGNED TO THIS MISSION AS WELL.
OF COURSE, MASTER ZYM. WE'LL LEAVE RIGHT AWAY.

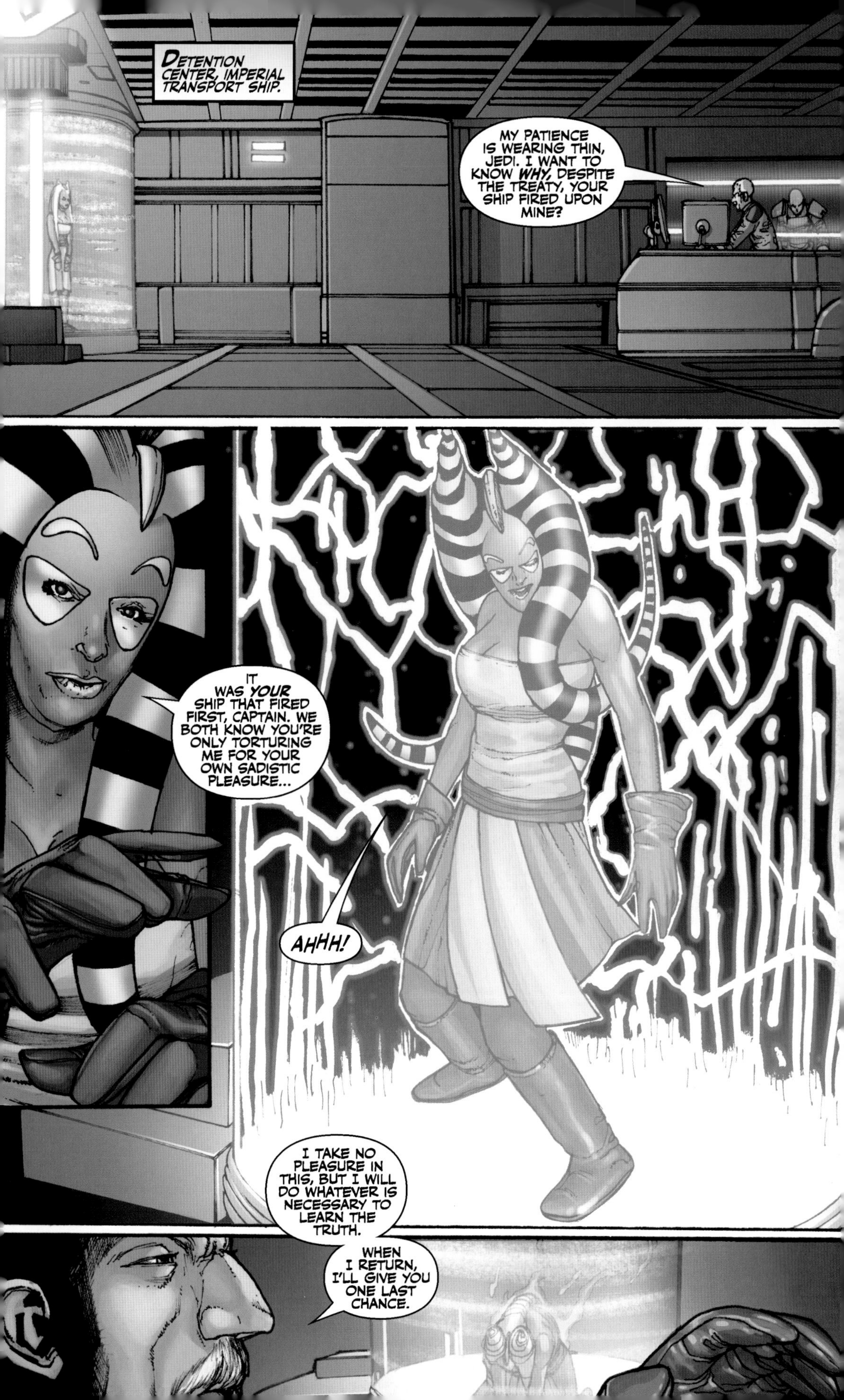
DETENTION CENTER, IMPERIAL TRANSPORT SHIP.
MY PATIENCE IS WEARING THIN, JEDI. I WANT TO KNOW WHY, DESPITE THE TREATY, YOUR SHIP FIRED UPON MINE?
IT WAS YOUR SHIP THAT FIRED FIRST, CAPTAIN. WE BOTH KNOW YOU'RE ONLY TORTURING ME FOR YOUR OWN SADISTIC PLEASURE...
AHHH!
I TAKE NO PLEASURE IN THIS, BUT I WILL DO WHATEVER IS NECESSARY TO LEARN THE TRUTH.
WHEN I RETURN, I'LL GIVE YOU ONE LAST CHANCE.

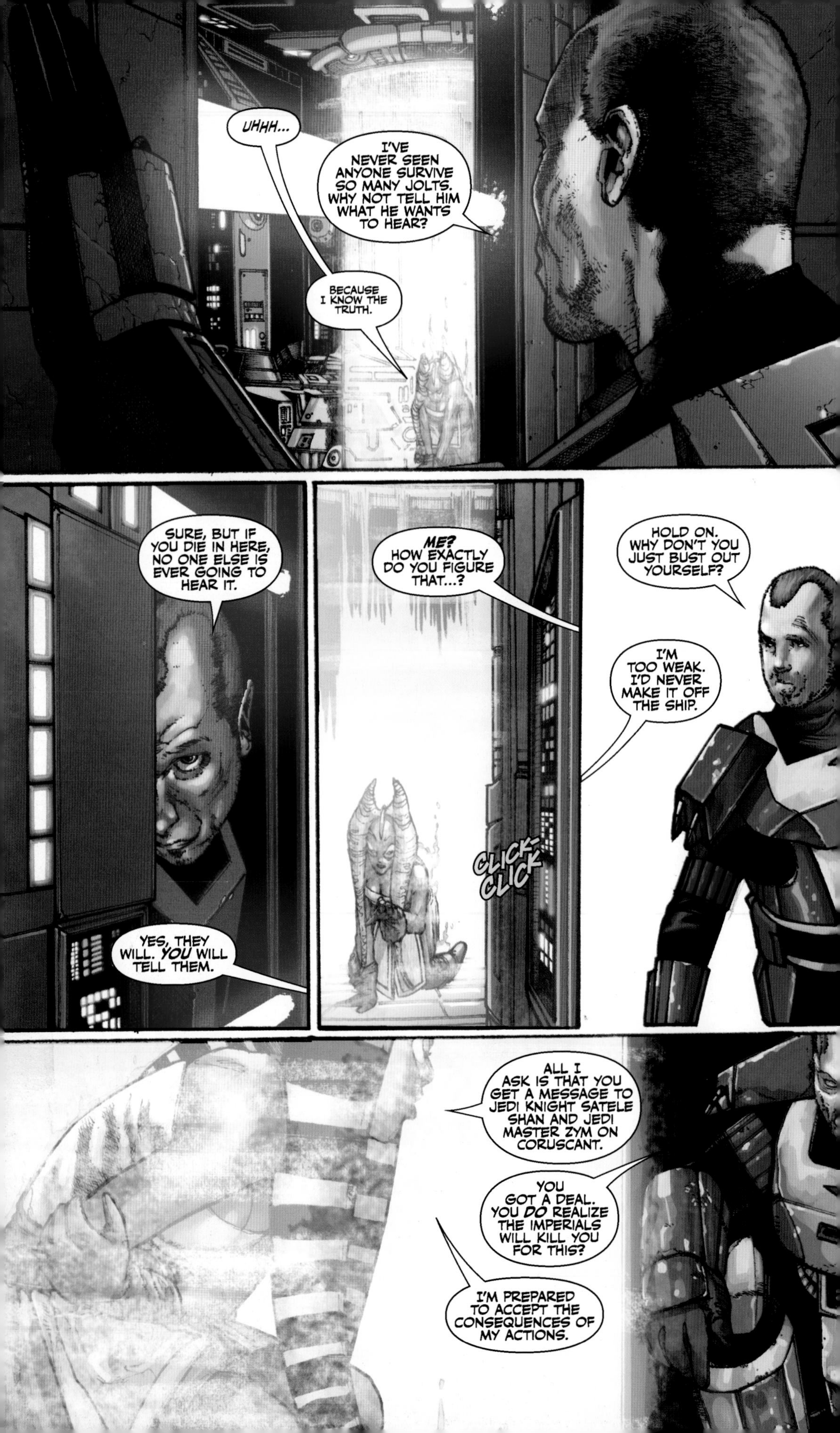
UHHH...
I'VE NEVER SEEN ANYONE SURVIVE SO MANY JOLTS. WHY NOT TELL HIM WHAT HE WANTS TO HEAR?
BECAUSE I KNOW THE TRUTH.
SURE, BUT IF YOU DIE IN HERE, NO ONE ELSE IS EVER GOING TO HEAR IT.
YES, THEY WILL. YOU WILL TELL THEM.
ME? HOW EXACTLY DO YOU FIGURE THAT...?
HOLD ON. WHY DON'T YOU JUST BUST OUT YOURSELF?
I'M TOO WEAK. I'D NEVER MAKE IT OFF THE SHIP.
CLICK-CLICK
ALL I ASK IS THAT YOU GET A MESSAGE TO JEDI KNIGHT SATELE SHAN AND JEDI MASTER ZYM ON CORUSCANT.
YOU GOT A DEAL. YOU DO REALIZE THE IMPERIALS WILL KILL YOU FOR THIS?
I'M PREPARED TO ACCEPT THE CONSEQUENCES OF MY ACTIONS.

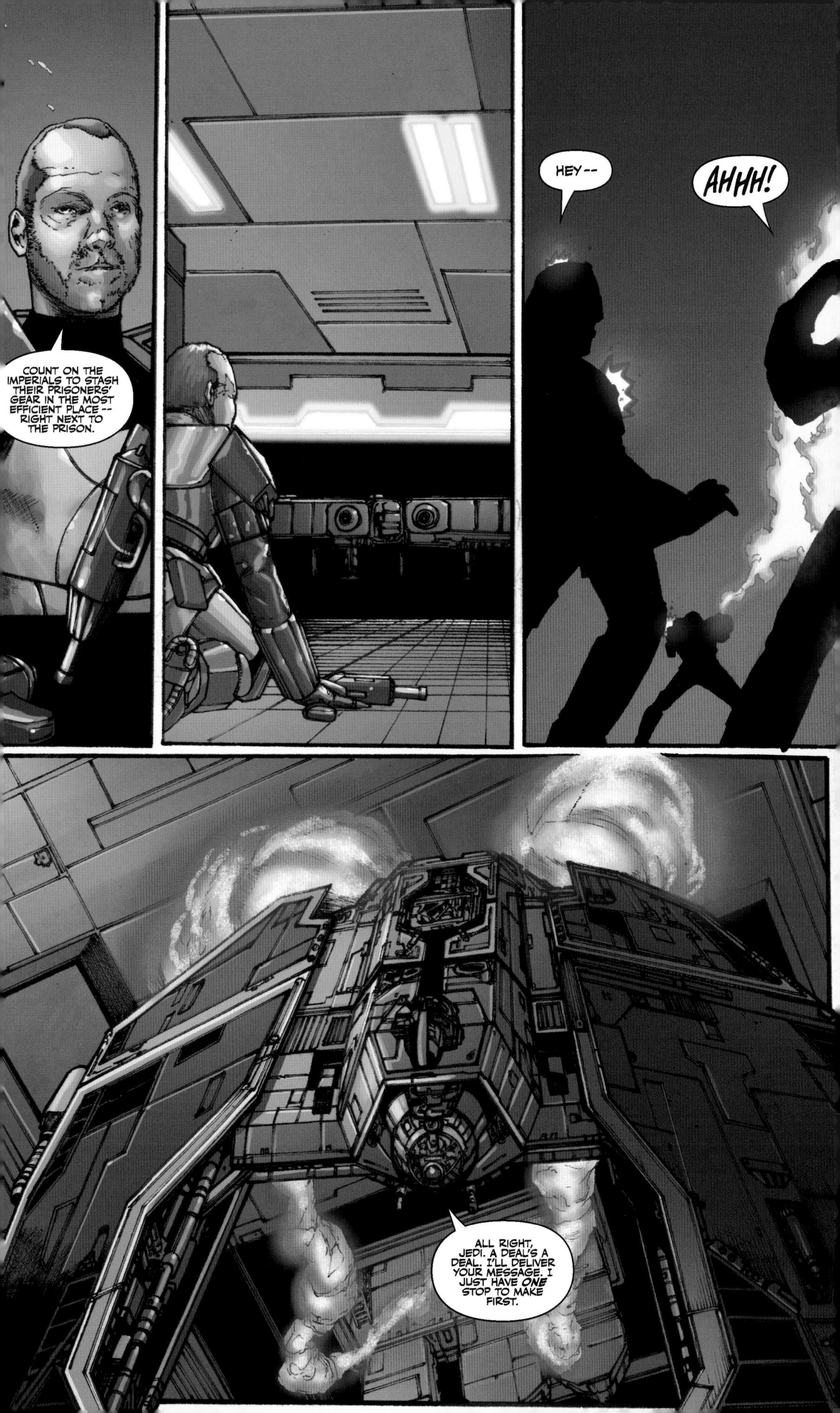
COUNT ON THE IMPERIALS TO STASH THEIR PRISONERS' GEAR IN THE MOST EFFICIENT PLACE -- RIGHT NEXT TO THE PRISON.
HEY--
AHHH!
ALL RIGHT, JEDI. A DEAL'S A DEAL. I'LL DELIVER YOUR MESSAGE. I JUST HAVE *ONE* STOP TO MAKE FIRST.

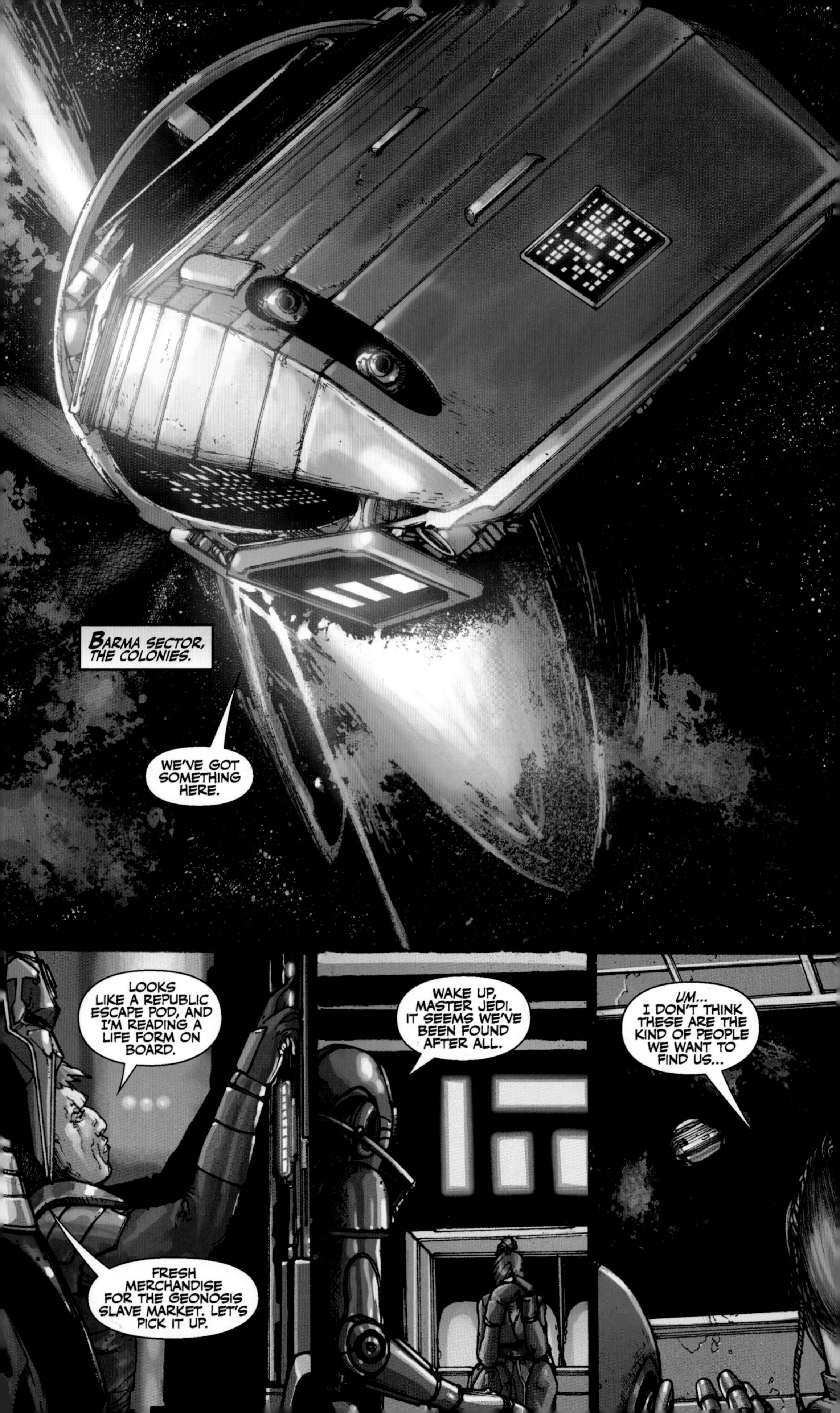
BARMA SECTOR, THE COLONIES.
WE'VE GOT SOMETHING HERE.
LOOKS LIKE A REPUBLIC ESCAPE POD, AND I'M READING A LIFE FORM ON BOARD.
FRESH MERCHANDISE FOR THE GEONOSIS SLAVE MARKET. LET'S PICK IT UP.
WAKE UP, MASTER JEDI. IT SEEMS WE'VE BEEN FOUND AFTER ALL.
UM... I DON'T THINK THESE ARE THE KIND OF PEOPLE WE WANT TO FIND US...

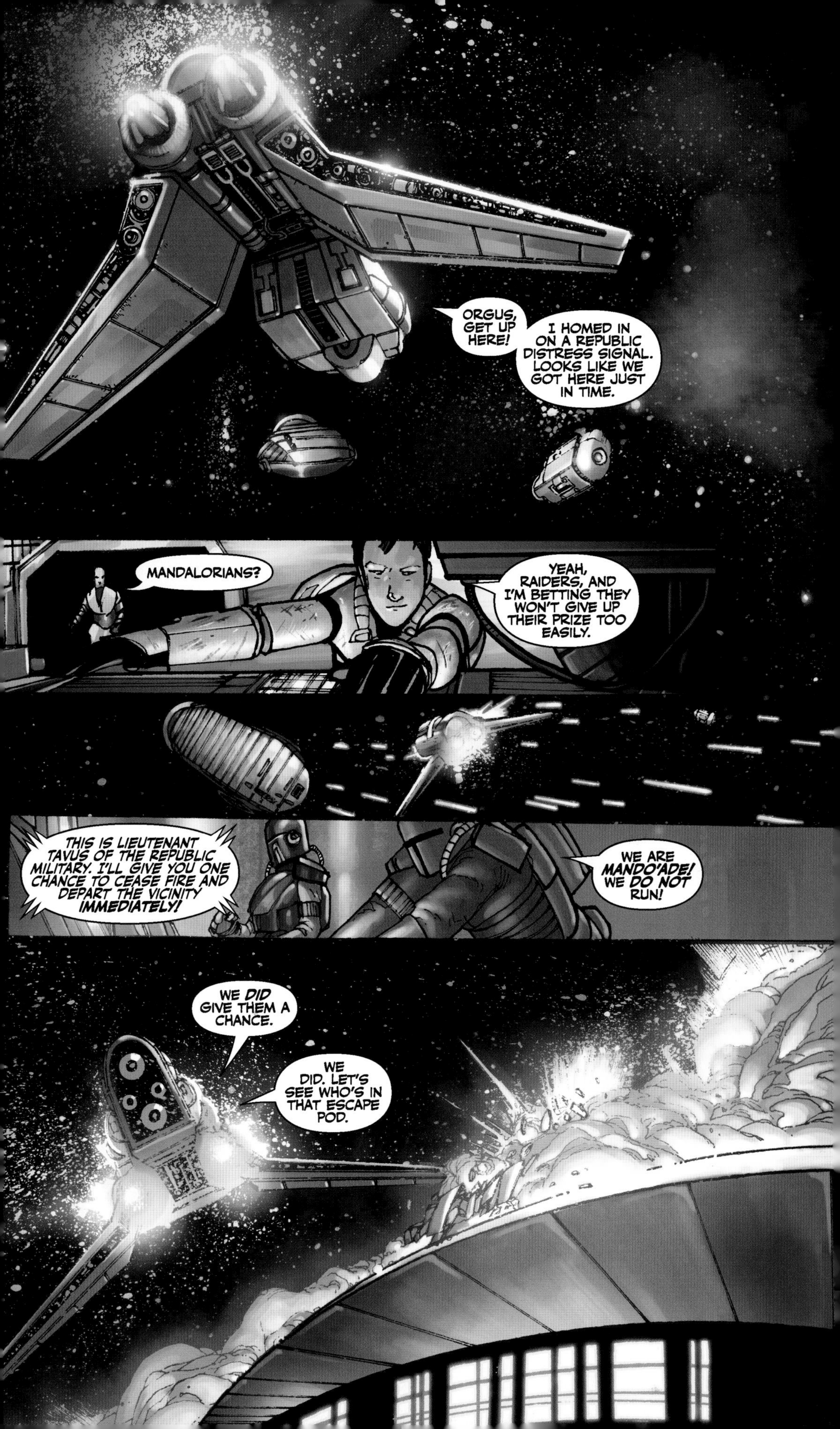
ORGUS, GET UP HERE!
I HOMED IN ON A REPUBLIC DISTRESS SIGNAL. LOOKS LIKE WE GOT HERE JUST IN TIME.
MANDALORIANS?
YEAH, RAIDERS, AND I'M BETTING THEY WON'T GIVE UP THEIR PRIZE TOO EASILY.
THIS IS LIEUTENANT TAVUS OF THE REPUBLIC MILITARY. I'LL GIVE YOU ONE CHANCE TO CEASE FIRE AND DEPART THE VICINITY IMMEDIATELY!
WE ARE MANDO'ADE! WE DO NOT RUN!
WE DID GIVE THEM A CHANCE.
WE DID. LET'S SEE WHO'S IN THAT ESCAPE POD.

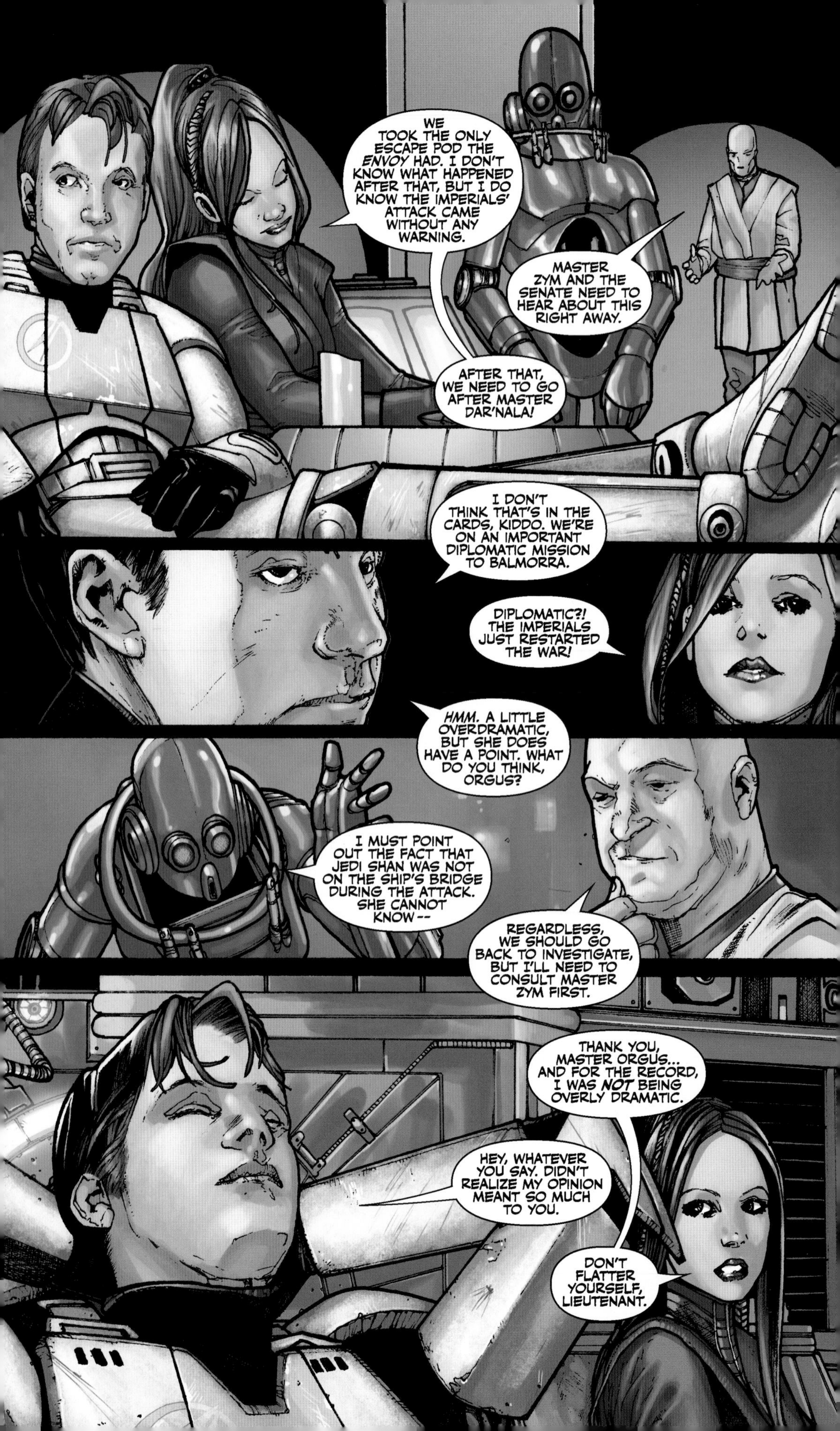
WE TOOK THE ONLY ESCAPE POD THE *ENVOY* HAD. I DON'T KNOW WHAT HAPPENED AFTER THAT, BUT I DO KNOW THE IMPERIALS' ATTACK CAME WITHOUT ANY WARNING.
MASTER ZYM AND THE SENATE NEED TO HEAR ABOUT THIS RIGHT AWAY.
AFTER THAT, WE NEED TO GO AFTER MASTER DAR'NALA!
I DON'T THINK THAT'S IN THE CARDS, KIDDO. WE'RE ON AN IMPORTANT DIPLOMATIC MISSION TO BALMORRA.
DIPLOMATIC?! THE IMPERIALS JUST RESTARTED THE WAR!
HMM. A LITTLE OVERDRAMATIC, BUT SHE DOES HAVE A POINT. WHAT DO YOU THINK, ORGUS?
I MUST POINT OUT THE FACT THAT JEDI SHAN WAS NOT ON THE SHIP'S BRIDGE DURING THE ATTACK. SHE CANNOT KNOW--
REGARDLESS, WE SHOULD GO BACK TO INVESTIGATE, BUT I'LL NEED TO CONSULT MASTER ZYM FIRST.
THANK YOU, MASTER ORGUS... AND FOR THE RECORD, I WAS *NOT* BEING OVERLY DRAMATIC.
HEY, WHATEVER YOU SAY. DIDN'T REALIZE MY OPINION MEANT SO MUCH TO YOU.
DON'T FLATTER YOURSELF, LIEUTENANT.

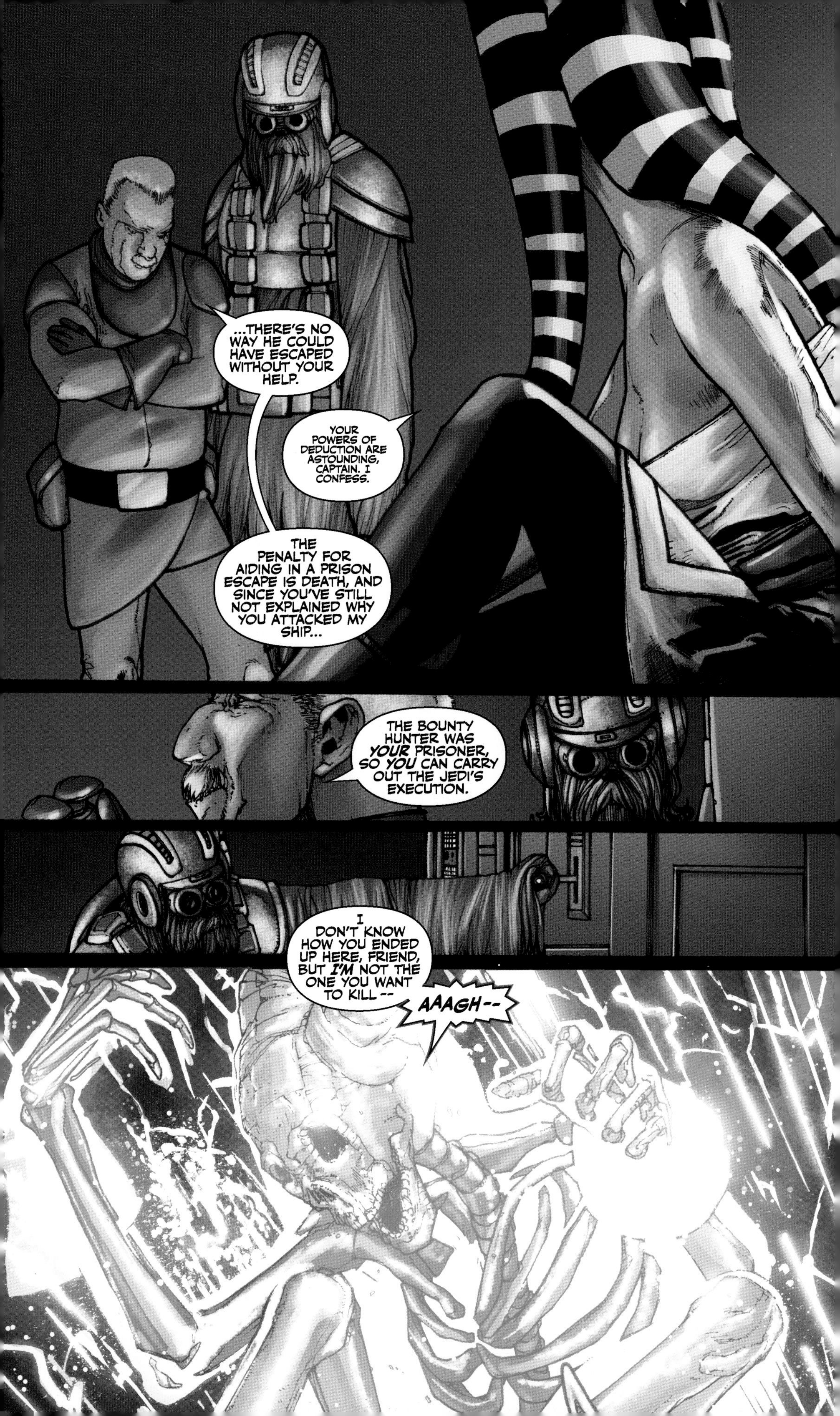
...THERE'S NO WAY HE COULD HAVE ESCAPED WITHOUT YOUR HELP.
YOUR POWERS OF DEDUCTION ARE ASTOUNDING, CAPTAIN. I CONFESS.
THE PENALTY FOR AIDING IN A PRISON ESCAPE IS DEATH, AND SINCE YOU'VE STILL NOT EXPLAINED WHY YOU ATTACKED MY SHIP...
THE BOUNTY HUNTER WAS *YOUR* PRISONER, SO *YOU* CAN CARRY OUT THE JEDI'S EXECUTION.
I DON'T KNOW HOW YOU ENDED UP HERE, FRIEND, BUT *I'M* NOT THE ONE YOU WANT TO KILL --
AAAGH --

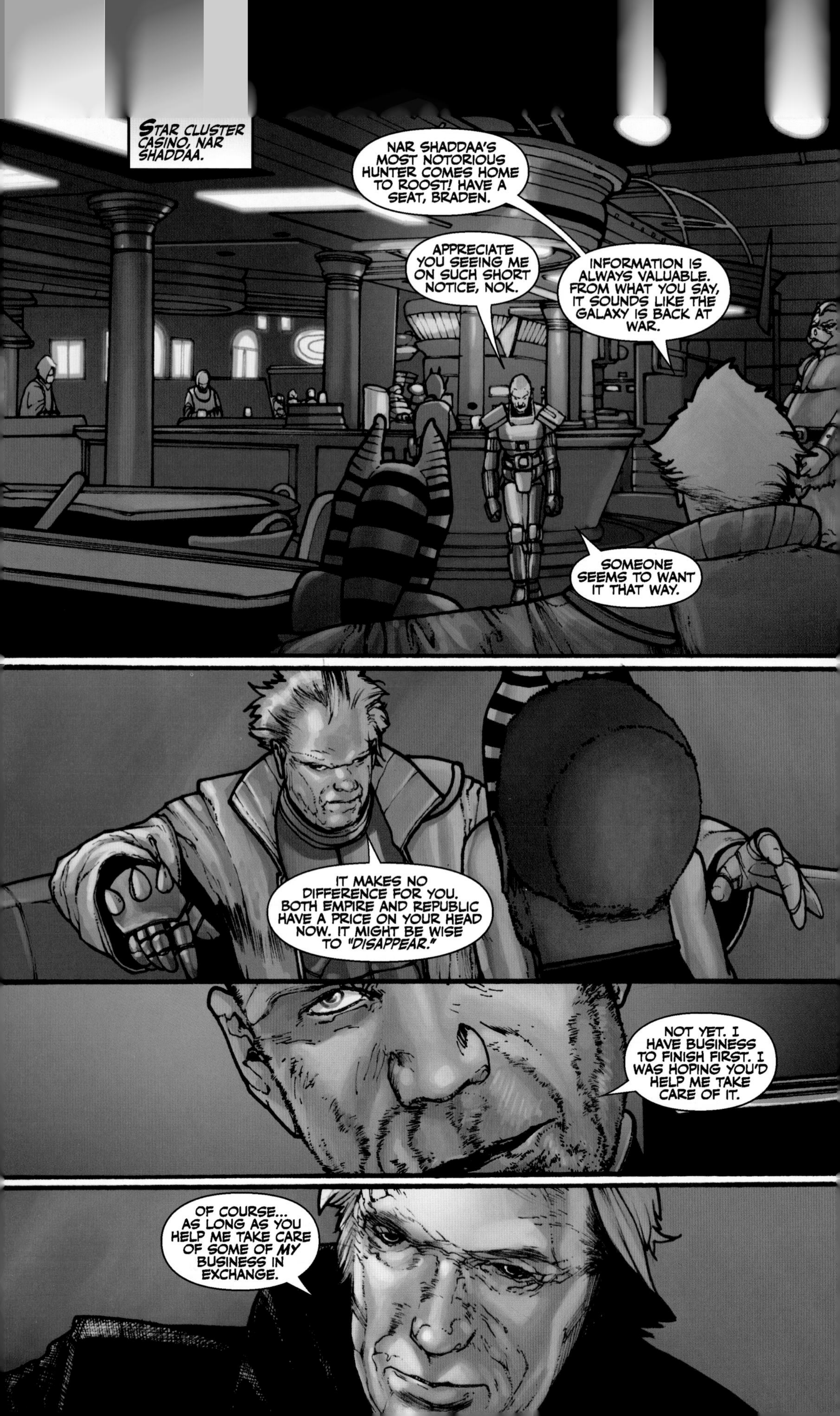
STAR CLUSTER CASINO, NAR SHADDAA.
NAR SHADDAA'S MOST NOTORIOUS HUNTER COMES HOME TO ROOST! HAVE A SEAT, BRADEN.
APPRECIATE YOU SEEING ME ON SUCH SHORT NOTICE, NOK.
INFORMATION IS ALWAYS VALUABLE. FROM WHAT YOU SAY, IT SOUNDS LIKE THE GALAXY IS BACK AT WAR.
SOMEONE SEEMS TO WANT IT THAT WAY.
IT MAKES NO DIFFERENCE FOR YOU. BOTH EMPIRE AND REPUBLIC HAVE A PRICE ON YOUR HEAD NOW. IT MIGHT BE WISE TO "DISAPPEAR."
NOT YET. I HAVE BUSINESS TO FINISH FIRST. I WAS HOPING YOU'D HELP ME TAKE CARE OF IT.
OF COURSE... AS LONG AS YOU HELP ME TAKE CARE OF SOME OF MY BUSINESS IN EXCHANGE.

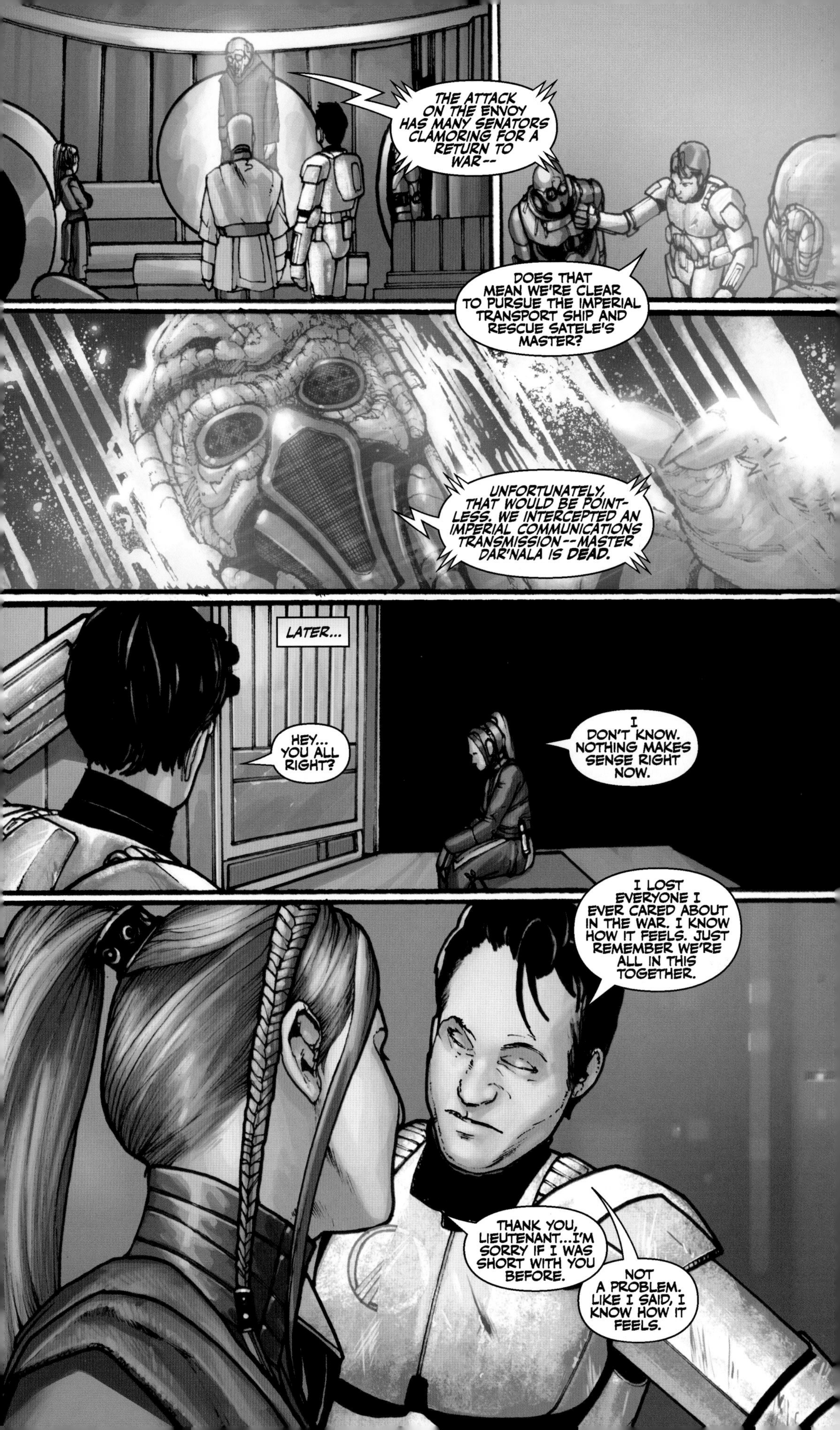
THE ATTACK ON THE ENVOY HAS MANY SENATORS CLAMORING FOR A RETURN TO WAR--
DOES THAT MEAN WE'RE CLEAR TO PURSUE THE IMPERIAL TRANSPORT SHIP AND RESCUE SATELE'S MASTER?
UNFORTUNATELY, THAT WOULD BE POINTLESS. WE INTERCEPTED AN IMPERIAL COMMUNICATIONS TRANSMISSION--MASTER DAR'NALA IS DEAD.
LATER...
HEY... YOU ALL RIGHT?
I DON'T KNOW. NOTHING MAKES SENSE RIGHT NOW.
I LOST EVERYONE I EVER CARED ABOUT IN THE WAR. I KNOW HOW IT FEELS. JUST REMEMBER WE'RE ALL IN THIS TOGETHER.
THANK YOU, LIEUTENANT...I'M SORRY IF I WAS SHORT WITH YOU BEFORE.
NOT A PROBLEM. LIKE I SAID, I KNOW HOW IT FEELS.

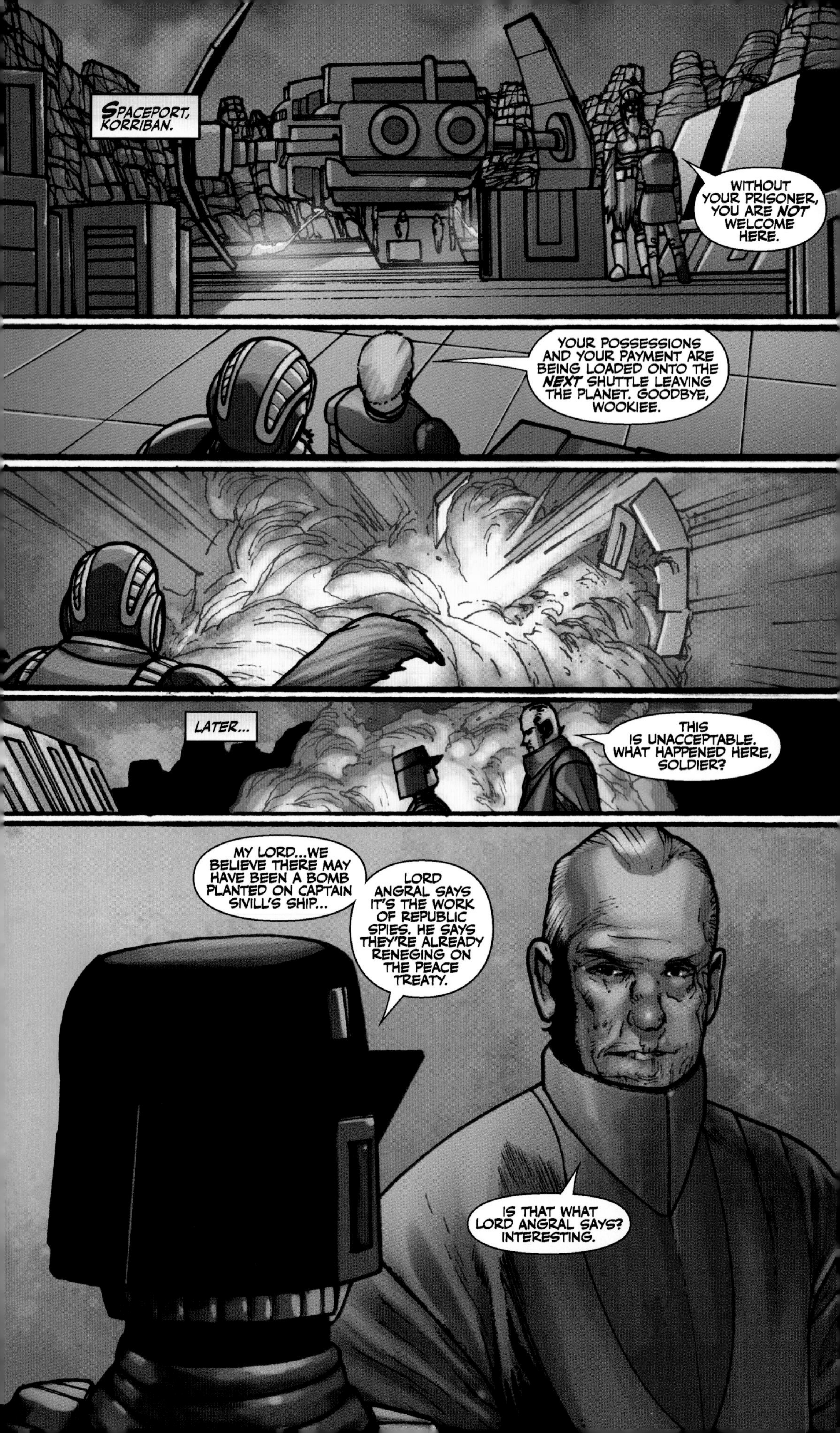
SPACEPORT, KORRIBAN.
WITHOUT YOUR PRISONER, YOU ARE *NOT* WELCOME HERE.
YOUR POSSESSIONS AND YOUR PAYMENT ARE BEING LOADED ONTO THE *NEXT* SHUTTLE LEAVING THE PLANET. GOODBYE, WOOKIEE.
LATER...
THIS IS UNACCEPTABLE. WHAT HAPPENED HERE, SOLDIER?
MY LORD...WE BELIEVE THERE MAY HAVE BEEN A BOMB PLANTED ON CAPTAIN SIVILL'S SHIP...
LORD ANGRAL SAYS IT'S THE WORK OF REPUBLIC SPIES. HE SAYS THEY'RE ALREADY RENEGING ON THE PEACE TREATY.
IS THAT WHAT LORD ANGRAL SAYS? INTERESTING.

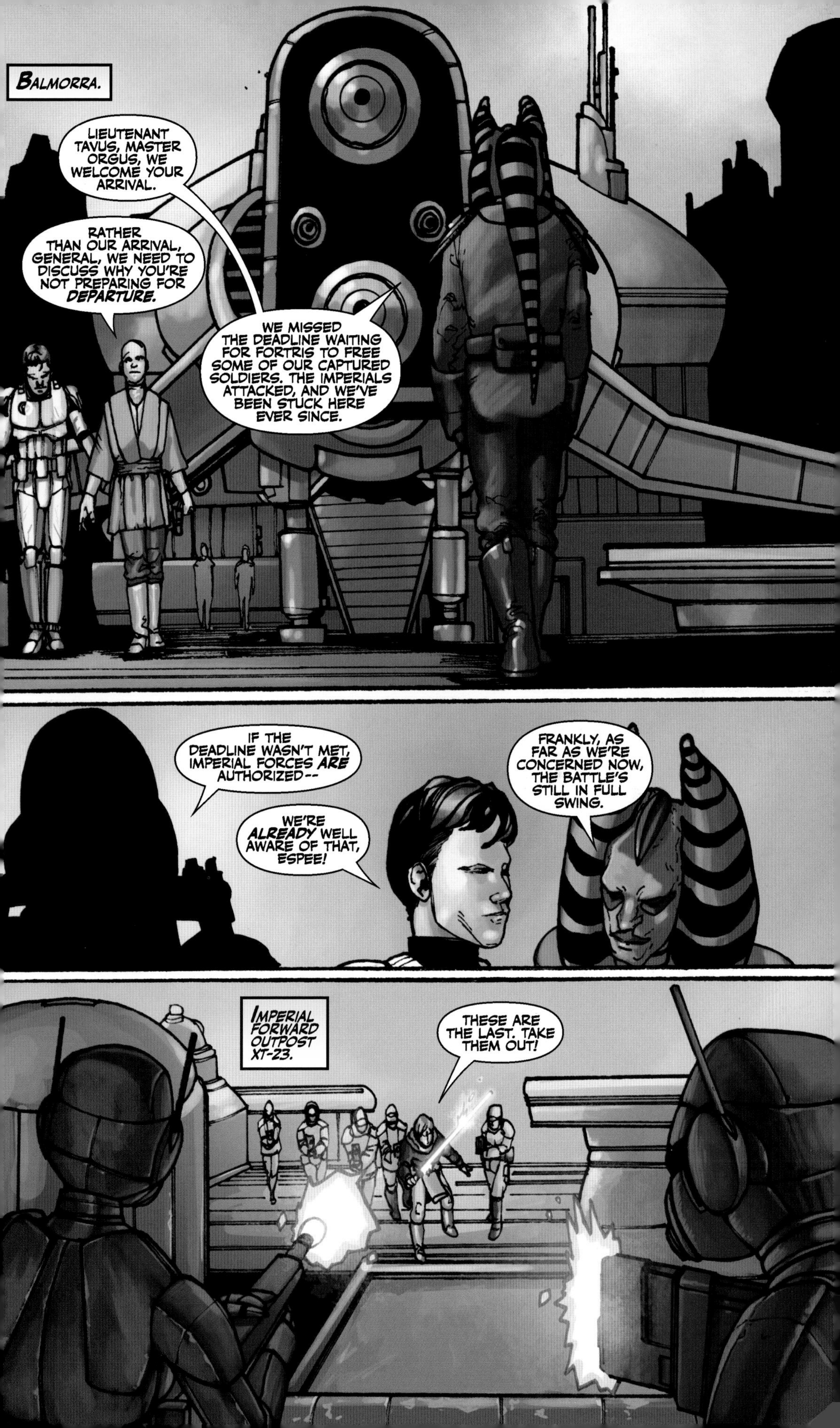
BALMORRA.
LIEUTENANT TAVUS, MASTER ORGUS, WE WELCOME YOUR ARRIVAL.
RATHER THAN OUR ARRIVAL, GENERAL, WE NEED TO DISCUSS WHY YOU'RE NOT PREPARING FOR DEPARTURE.
WE MISSED THE DEADLINE WAITING FOR FORTRIS TO FREE SOME OF OUR CAPTURED SOLDIERS. THE IMPERIALS ATTACKED, AND WE'VE BEEN STUCK HERE EVER SINCE.
IF THE DEADLINE WASN'T MET, IMPERIAL FORCES ARE AUTHORIZED--
WE'RE ALREADY WELL AWARE OF THAT, ESPEE!
FRANKLY, AS FAR AS WE'RE CONCERNED NOW, THE BATTLE'S STILL IN FULL SWING.
IMPERIAL FORWARD OUTPOST XT-23.
THESE ARE THE LAST. TAKE THEM OUT!

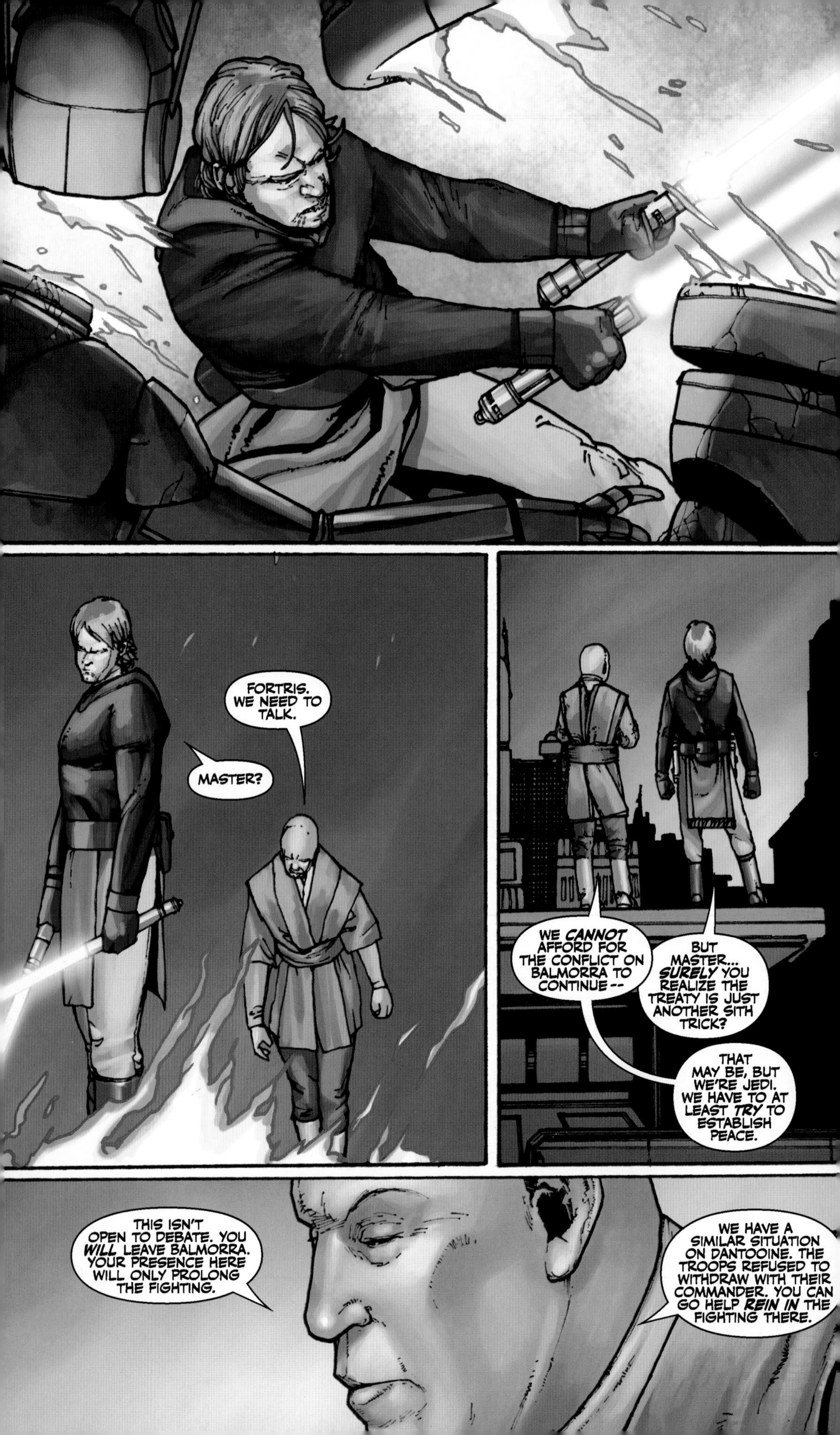
FORTRIS. WE NEED TO TALK.
MASTER?
WE CANNOT AFFORD FOR THE CONFLICT ON BALMORRA TO CONTINUE --
BUT MASTER... SURELY YOU REALIZE THE TREATY IS JUST ANOTHER SITH TRICK?
THAT MAY BE, BUT WE'RE JEDI. WE HAVE TO AT LEAST TRY TO ESTABLISH PEACE.
THIS ISN'T OPEN TO DEBATE. YOU WILL LEAVE BALMORRA. YOUR PRESENCE HERE WILL ONLY PROLONG THE FIGHTING.
WE HAVE A SIMILAR SITUATION ON DANTOOINE. THE TROOPS REFUSED TO WITHDRAW WITH THEIR COMMANDER. YOU CAN GO HELP REIN IN THE FIGHTING THERE.

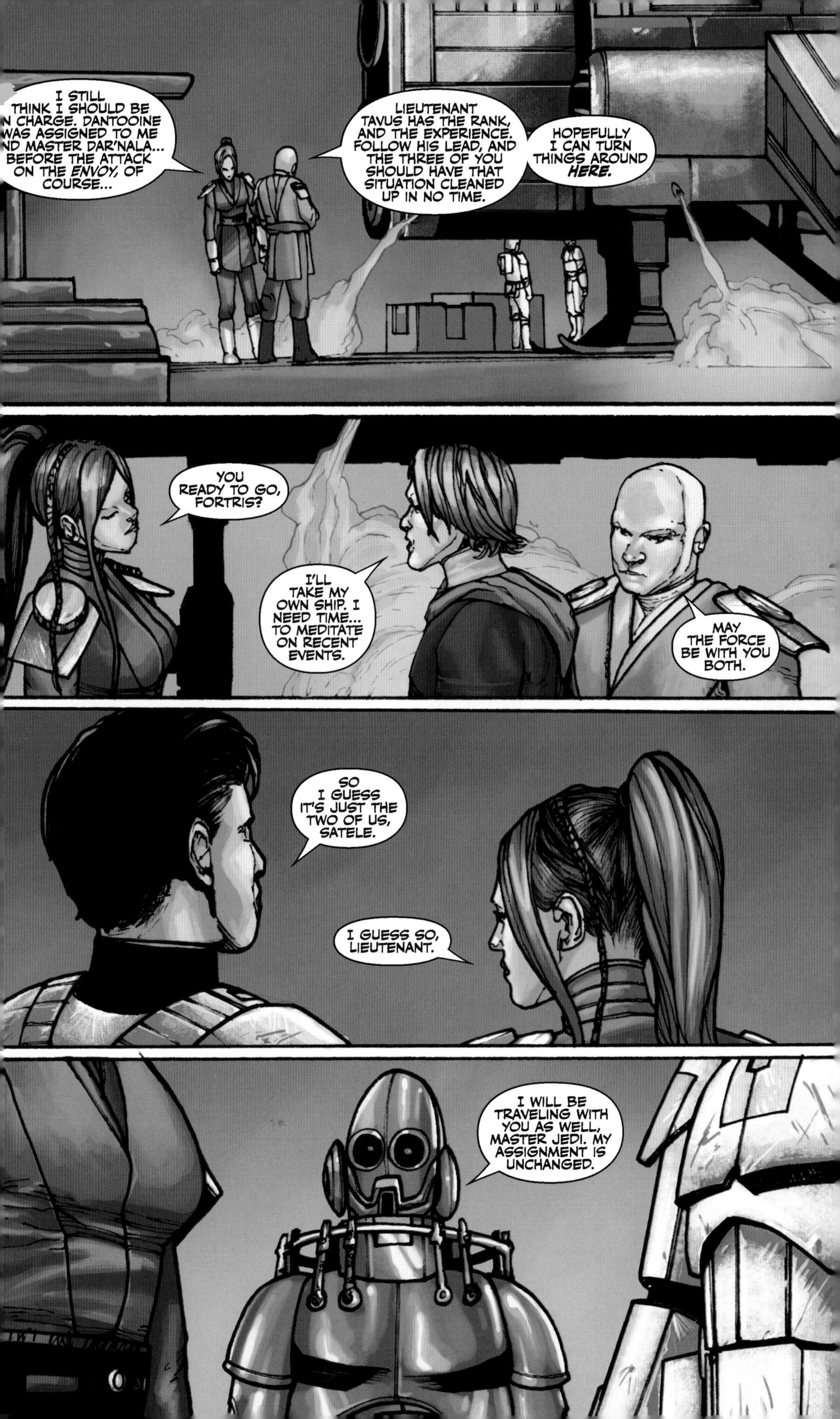
I STILL THINK I SHOULD BE N CHARGE. DANTOOINE WAS ASSIGNED TO ME ND MASTER DAR'NALA... BEFORE THE ATTACK ON THE *ENVOY*, OF COURSE...
LIEUTENANT TAVUS HAS THE RANK, AND THE EXPERIENCE. FOLLOW HIS LEAD, AND THE THREE OF YOU SHOULD HAVE THAT SITUATION CLEANED UP IN NO TIME.
HOPEFULLY I CAN TURN THINGS AROUND ***HERE.***
YOU READY TO GO, FORTRIS?
I'LL TAKE MY OWN SHIP. I NEED TIME... TO MEDITATE ON RECENT EVENTS.
MAY THE FORCE BE WITH YOU BOTH.
SO I GUESS IT'S JUST THE TWO OF US, SATELE.
I GUESS SO, LIEUTENANT.
I WILL BE TRAVELING WITH YOU AS WELL, MASTER JEDI. MY ASSIGNMENT IS UNCHANGED.

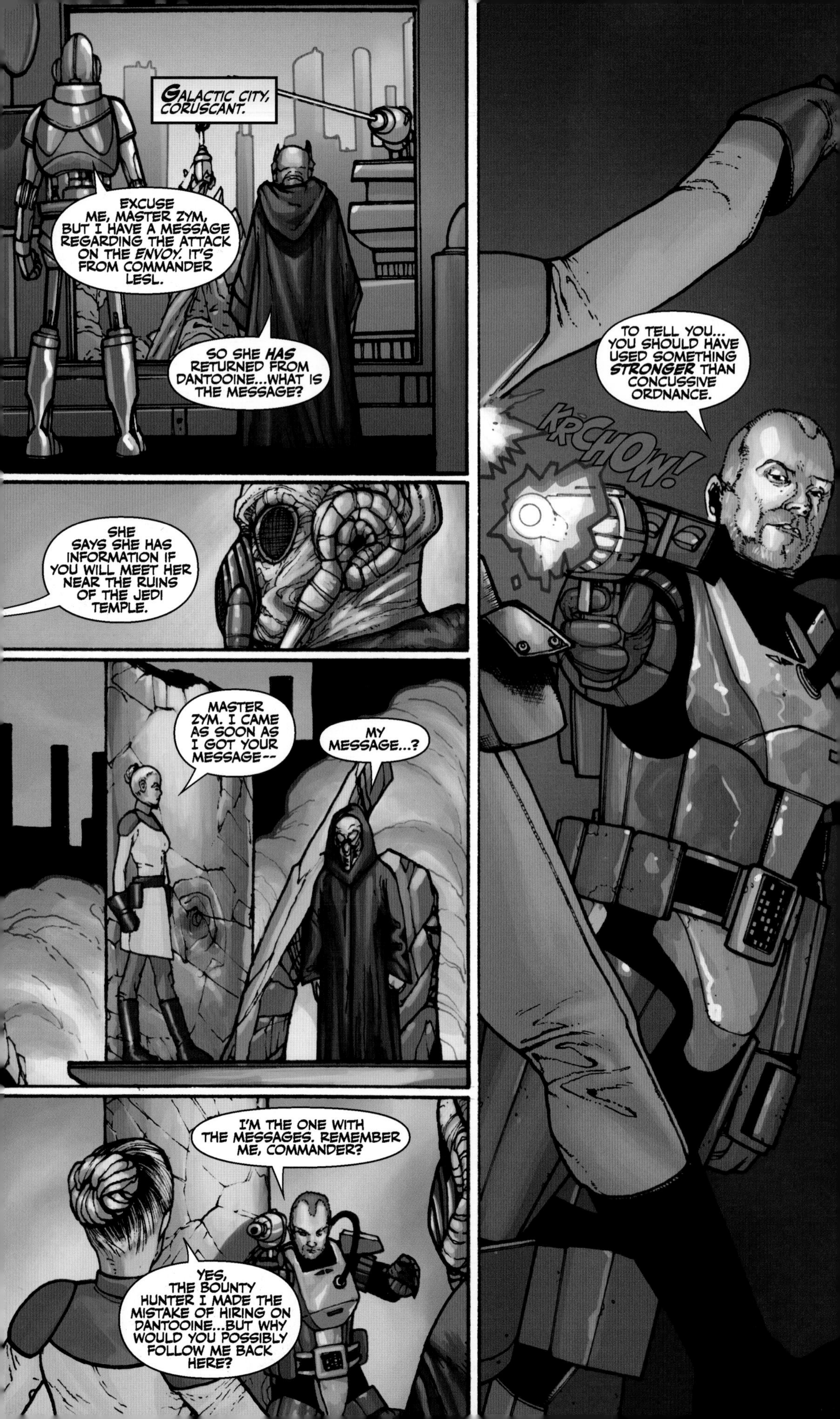
GALACTIC CITY, CORUSCANT.
EXCUSE ME, MASTER ZYM, BUT I HAVE A MESSAGE REGARDING THE ATTACK ON THE *ENVOY*. IT'S FROM COMMANDER LESL.
SO SHE *HAS* RETURNED FROM DANTOOINE...WHAT IS THE MESSAGE?
SHE SAYS SHE HAS INFORMATION IF YOU WILL MEET HER NEAR THE RUINS OF THE JEDI TEMPLE.
MASTER ZYM. I CAME AS SOON AS I GOT YOUR MESSAGE--
MY MESSAGE...?
I'M THE ONE WITH THE MESSAGES. REMEMBER ME, COMMANDER?
YES, THE BOUNTY HUNTER I MADE THE MISTAKE OF HIRING ON DANTOOINE...BUT WHY WOULD YOU POSSIBLY FOLLOW ME BACK HERE?
TO TELL YOU... YOU SHOULD HAVE USED SOMETHING *STRONGER* THAN CONCUSSIVE ORDNANCE.
KRCHOW!

NO SCORE TO SETTLE WITH YOU, JEDI...MY MESSAGE FOR YOU IS FROM ONE OF YOUR FORMER COLLEAGUES...

PUT DOWN THE BLASTER THEN. YOU CAN GIVE ME THE MESSAGE *AFTER* I'VE PLACED YOU UNDER ARREST.

I WAS DOING YOU A FAVOR, BUT HAVE IT YOUR WAY!

UHH!

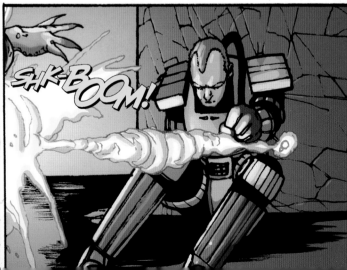

SHK-BOOM!

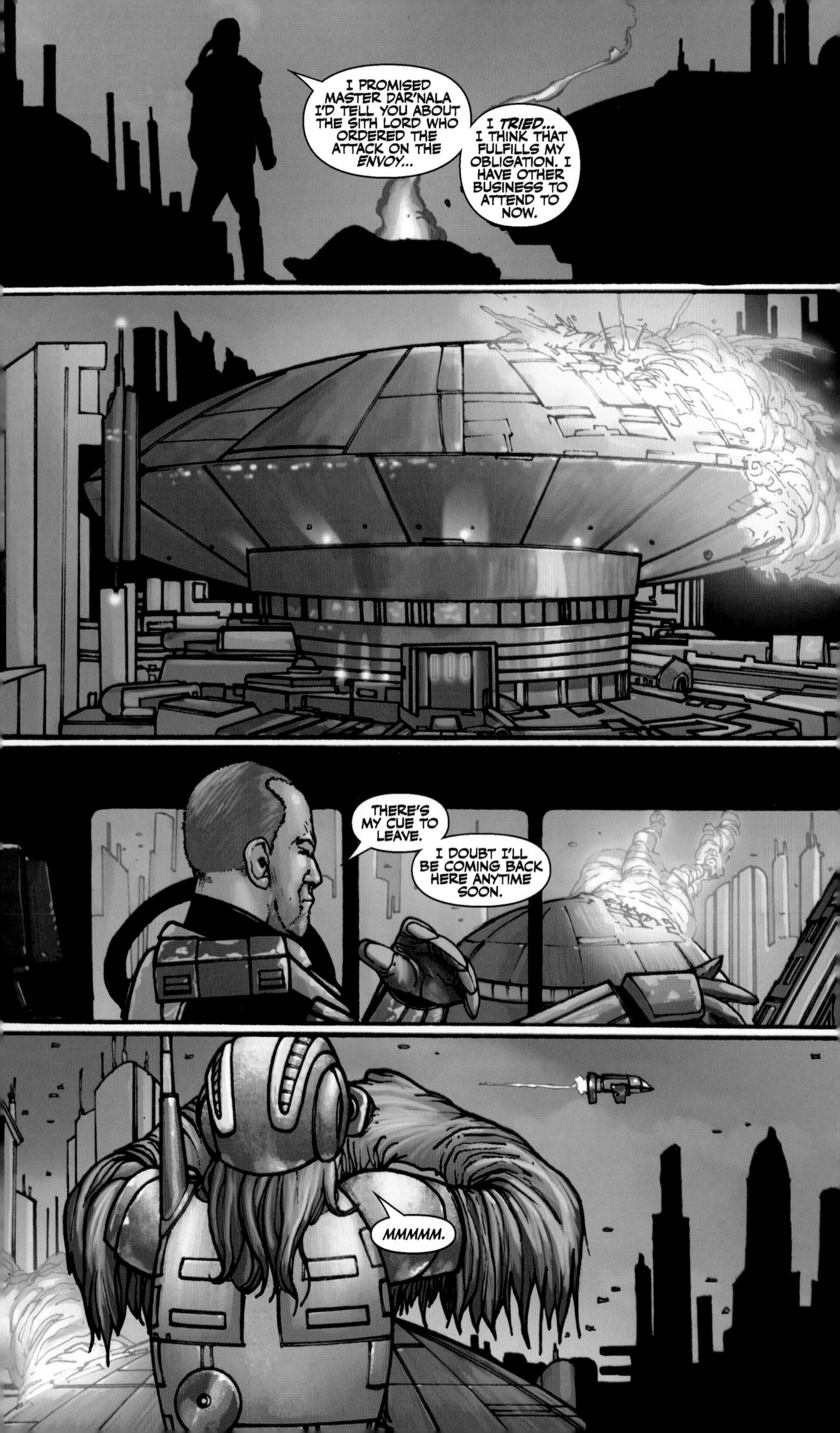
I PROMISED MASTER DAR'NALA I'D TELL YOU ABOUT THE SITH LORD WHO ORDERED THE ATTACK ON THE *ENVOY*...
I *TRIED*... I THINK THAT FULFILLS MY OBLIGATION. I HAVE OTHER BUSINESS TO ATTEND TO NOW.
THERE'S MY CUE TO LEAVE.
I DOUBT I'LL BE COMING BACK HERE ANYTIME SOON.
MMMMM.

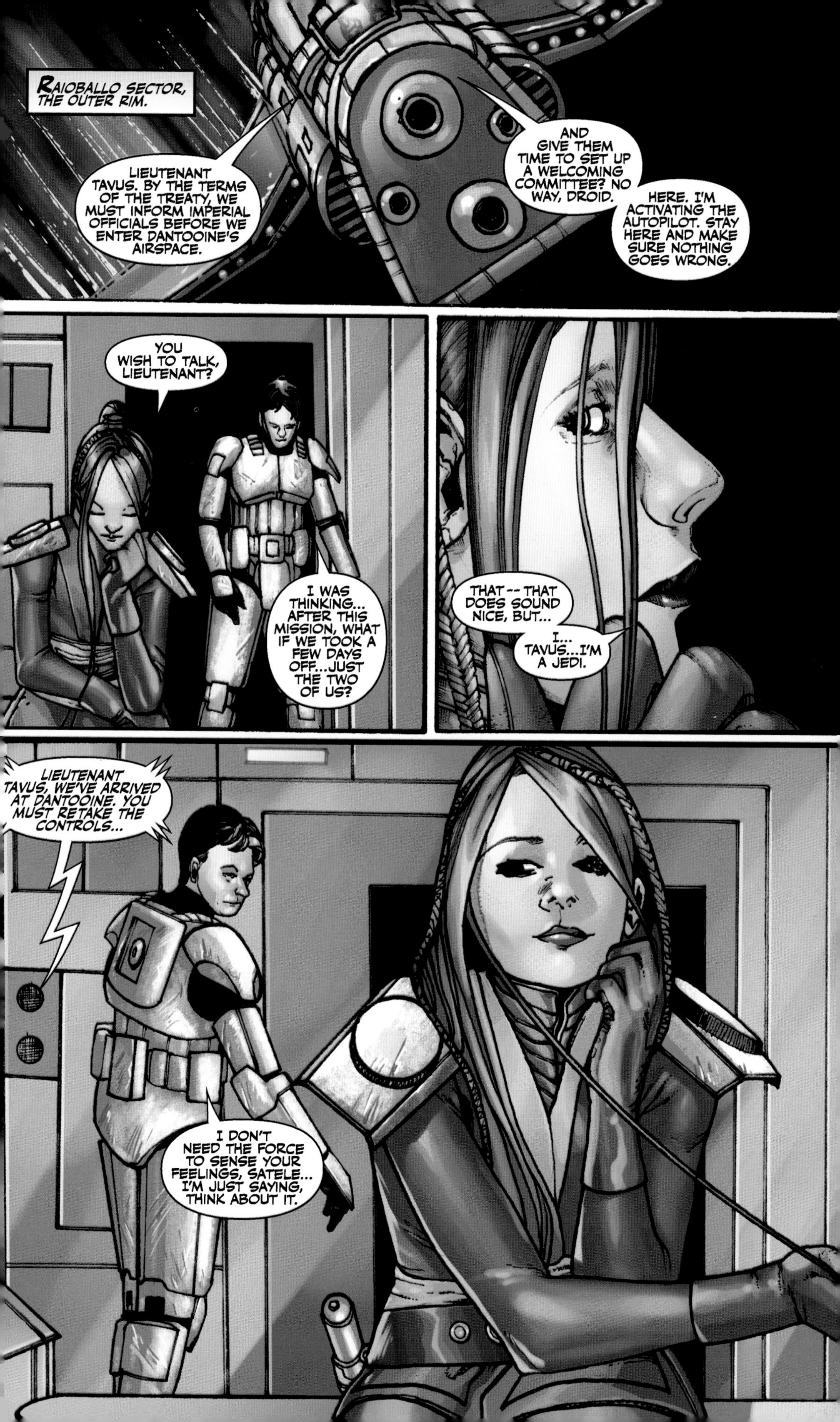
RAIOBALLO SECTOR, THE OUTER RIM.
LIEUTENANT TAVUS. BY THE TERMS OF THE TREATY, WE MUST INFORM IMPERIAL OFFICIALS BEFORE WE ENTER DANTOOINE'S AIRSPACE.
AND GIVE THEM TIME TO SET UP A WELCOMING COMMITTEE? NO WAY, DROID.
HERE. I'M ACTIVATING THE AUTOPILOT. STAY HERE AND MAKE SURE NOTHING GOES WRONG.
YOU WISH TO TALK, LIEUTENANT?
I WAS THINKING... AFTER THIS MISSION, WHAT IF WE TOOK A FEW DAYS OFF...JUST THE TWO OF US?
THAT -- THAT DOES SOUND NICE, BUT...
I... TAVUS...I'M A JEDI.
LIEUTENANT TAVUS, WE'VE ARRIVED AT DANTOOINE. YOU MUST RETAKE THE CONTROLS...
I DON'T NEED THE FORCE TO SENSE YOUR FEELINGS, SATELE... I'M JUST SAYING, THINK ABOUT IT.

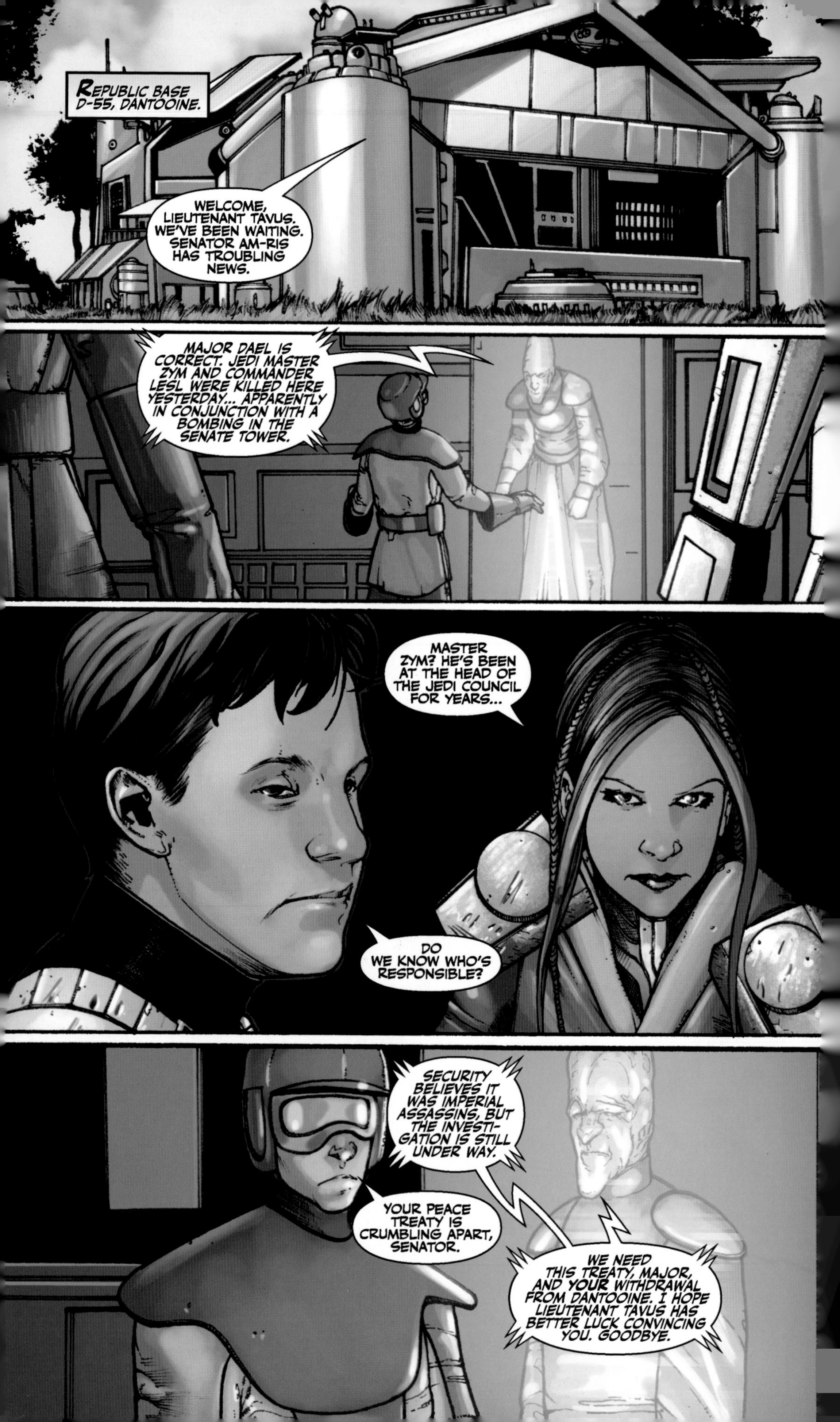
REPUBLIC BASE D-55, DANTOOINE.
WELCOME, LIEUTENANT TAVUS. WE'VE BEEN WAITING. SENATOR AM-RIS HAS TROUBLING NEWS.
MAJOR DAEL IS CORRECT. JEDI MASTER ZYM AND COMMANDER LESL WERE KILLED HERE YESTERDAY... APPARENTLY IN CONJUNCTION WITH A BOMBING IN THE SENATE TOWER.
MASTER ZYM? HE'S BEEN AT THE HEAD OF THE JEDI COUNCIL FOR YEARS...
DO WE KNOW WHO'S RESPONSIBLE?
SECURITY BELIEVES IT WAS IMPERIAL ASSASSINS, BUT THE INVESTI-GATION IS STILL UNDER WAY.
YOUR PEACE TREATY IS CRUMBLING APART, SENATOR.
WE NEED THIS TREATY, MAJOR, AND YOUR WITHDRAWAL FROM DANTOOINE. I HOPE LIEUTENANT TAVUS HAS BETTER LUCK CONVINCING YOU. GOODBYE.

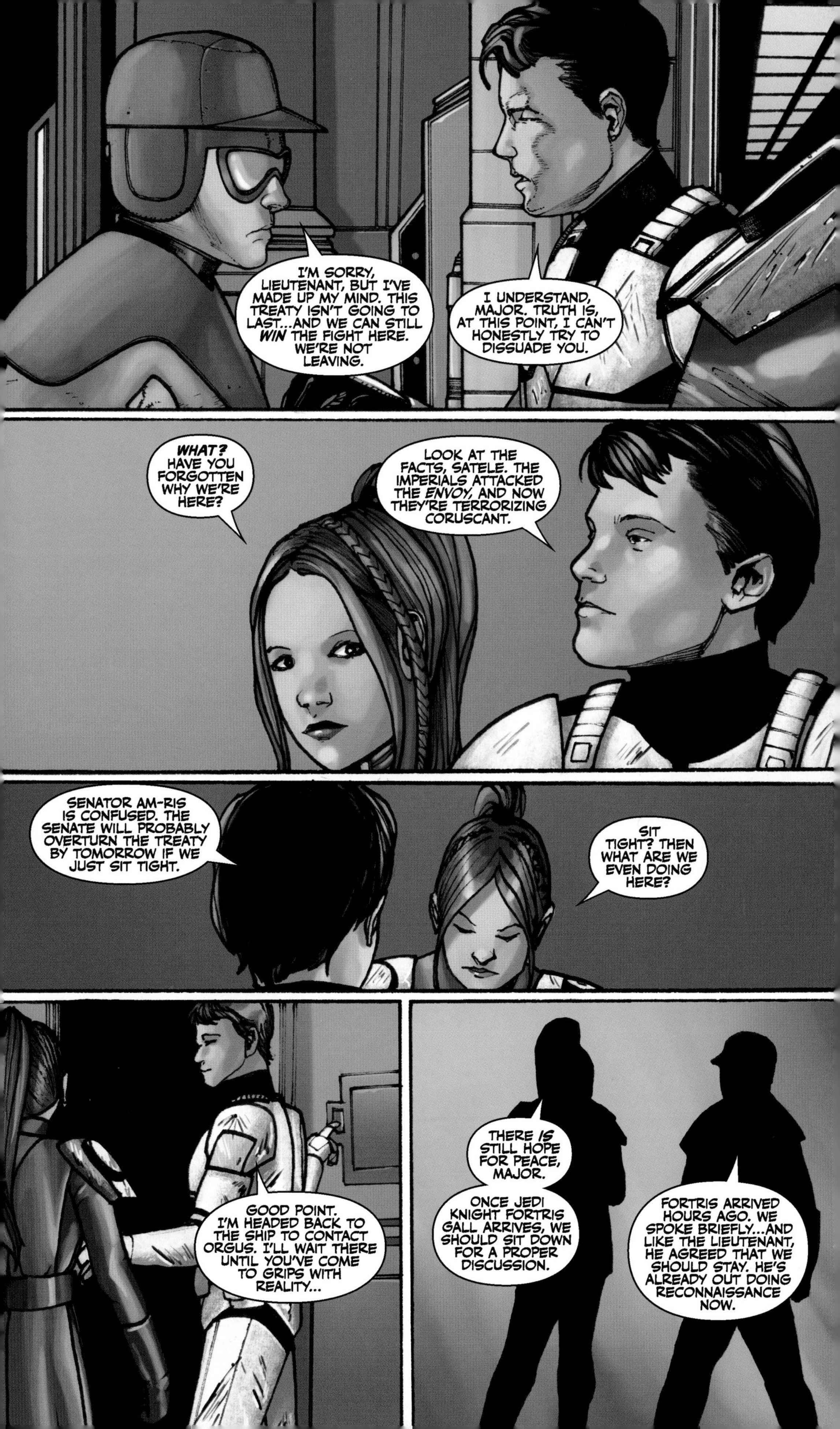
I'M SORRY, LIEUTENANT, BUT I'VE MADE UP MY MIND. THIS TREATY ISN'T GOING TO LAST...AND WE CAN STILL *WIN* THE FIGHT HERE. WE'RE NOT LEAVING.
I UNDERSTAND, MAJOR. TRUTH IS, AT THIS POINT, I CAN'T HONESTLY TRY TO DISSUADE YOU.
WHAT? HAVE YOU FORGOTTEN WHY WE'RE HERE?
LOOK AT THE FACTS, SATELE. THE IMPERIALS ATTACKED THE *ENVOY,* AND NOW THEY'RE TERRORIZING CORUSCANT.
SENATOR AM-RIS IS CONFUSED. THE SENATE WILL PROBABLY OVERTURN THE TREATY BY TOMORROW IF WE JUST SIT TIGHT.
SIT TIGHT? THEN WHAT ARE WE EVEN DOING HERE?
GOOD POINT. I'M HEADED BACK TO THE SHIP TO CONTACT ORGUS. I'LL WAIT THERE UNTIL YOU'VE COME TO GRIPS WITH REALITY...
THERE *IS* STILL HOPE FOR PEACE, MAJOR.
ONCE JEDI KNIGHT FORTRIS GALL ARRIVES, WE SHOULD SIT DOWN FOR A PROPER DISCUSSION.
FORTRIS ARRIVED HOURS AGO. WE SPOKE BRIEFLY...AND LIKE THE LIEUTENANT, HE AGREED THAT WE SHOULD STAY. HE'S ALREADY OUT DOING RECONNAISSANCE NOW.

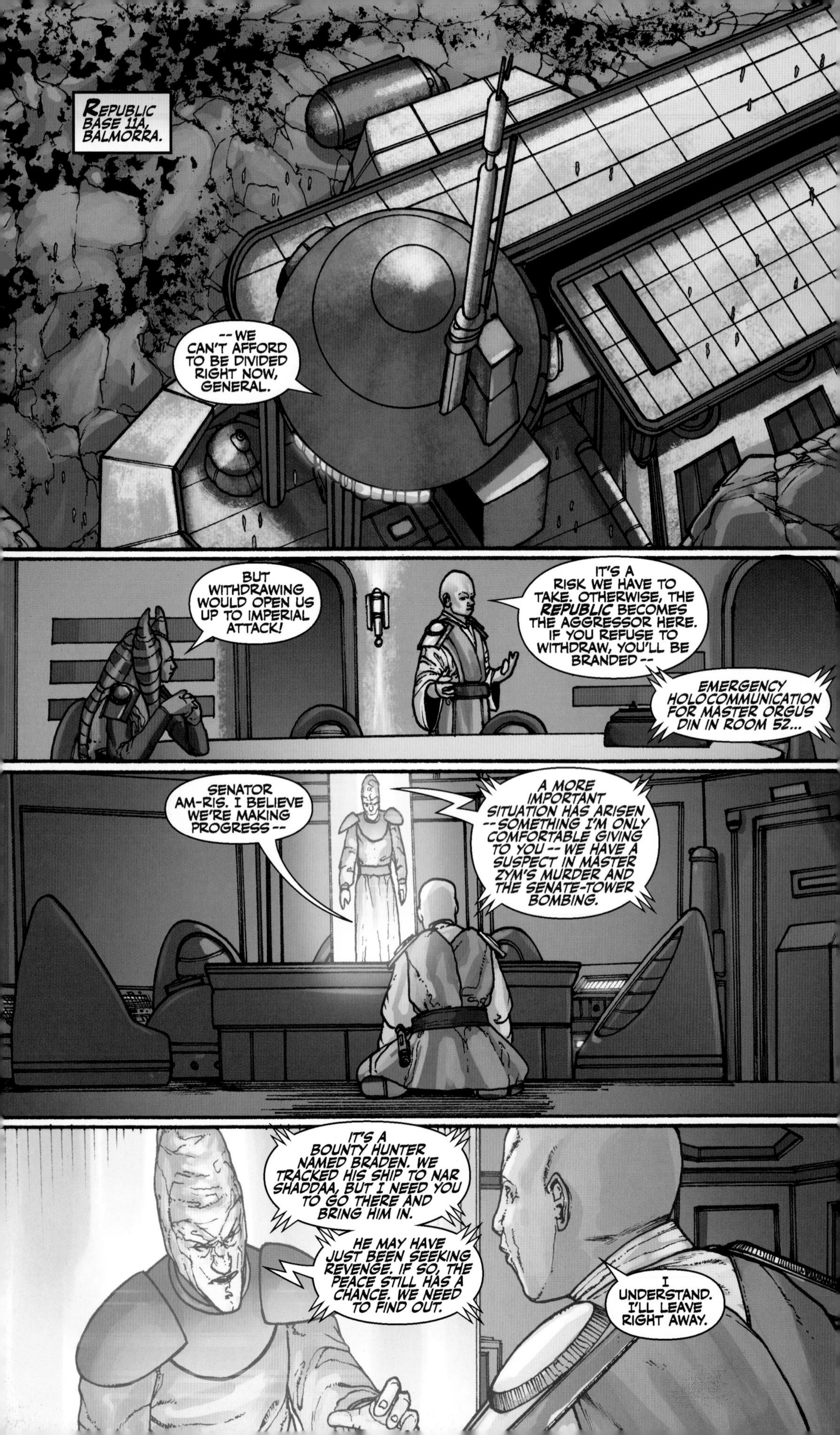
REPUBLIC BASE 11A, BALMORRA.
--WE CAN'T AFFORD TO BE DIVIDED RIGHT NOW, GENERAL.
BUT WITHDRAWING WOULD OPEN US UP TO IMPERIAL ATTACK!
IT'S A RISK WE HAVE TO TAKE. OTHERWISE, THE REPUBLIC BECOMES THE AGGRESSOR HERE. IF YOU REFUSE TO WITHDRAW, YOU'LL BE BRANDED--
EMERGENCY HOLOCOMMUNICATION FOR MASTER ORGUS DIN IN ROOM 52...
SENATOR AM-RIS. I BELIEVE WE'RE MAKING PROGRESS--
A MORE IMPORTANT SITUATION HAS ARISEN --SOMETHING I'M ONLY COMFORTABLE GIVING TO YOU-- WE HAVE A SUSPECT IN MASTER ZYM'S MURDER AND THE SENATE-TOWER BOMBING.
IT'S A BOUNTY HUNTER NAMED BRADEN. WE TRACKED HIS SHIP TO NAR SHADDAA, BUT I NEED YOU TO GO THERE AND BRING HIM IN.
HE MAY HAVE JUST BEEN SEEKING REVENGE. IF SO, THE PEACE STILL HAS A CHANCE. WE NEED TO FIND OUT.
I UNDERSTAND. I'LL LEAVE RIGHT AWAY.

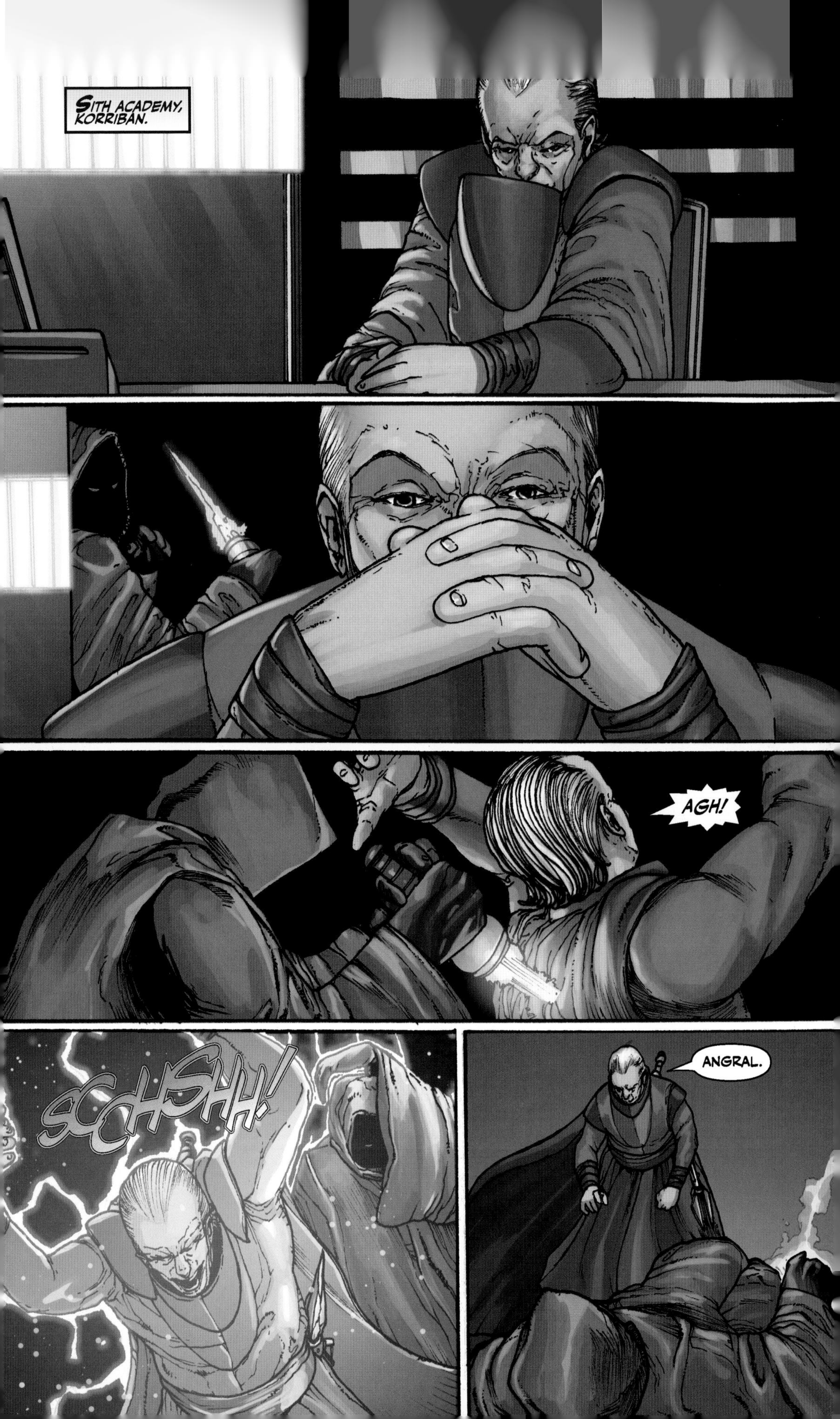
SITH ACADEMY, KORRIBAN.
AGH!
SCCHSHH!
ANGRAL.

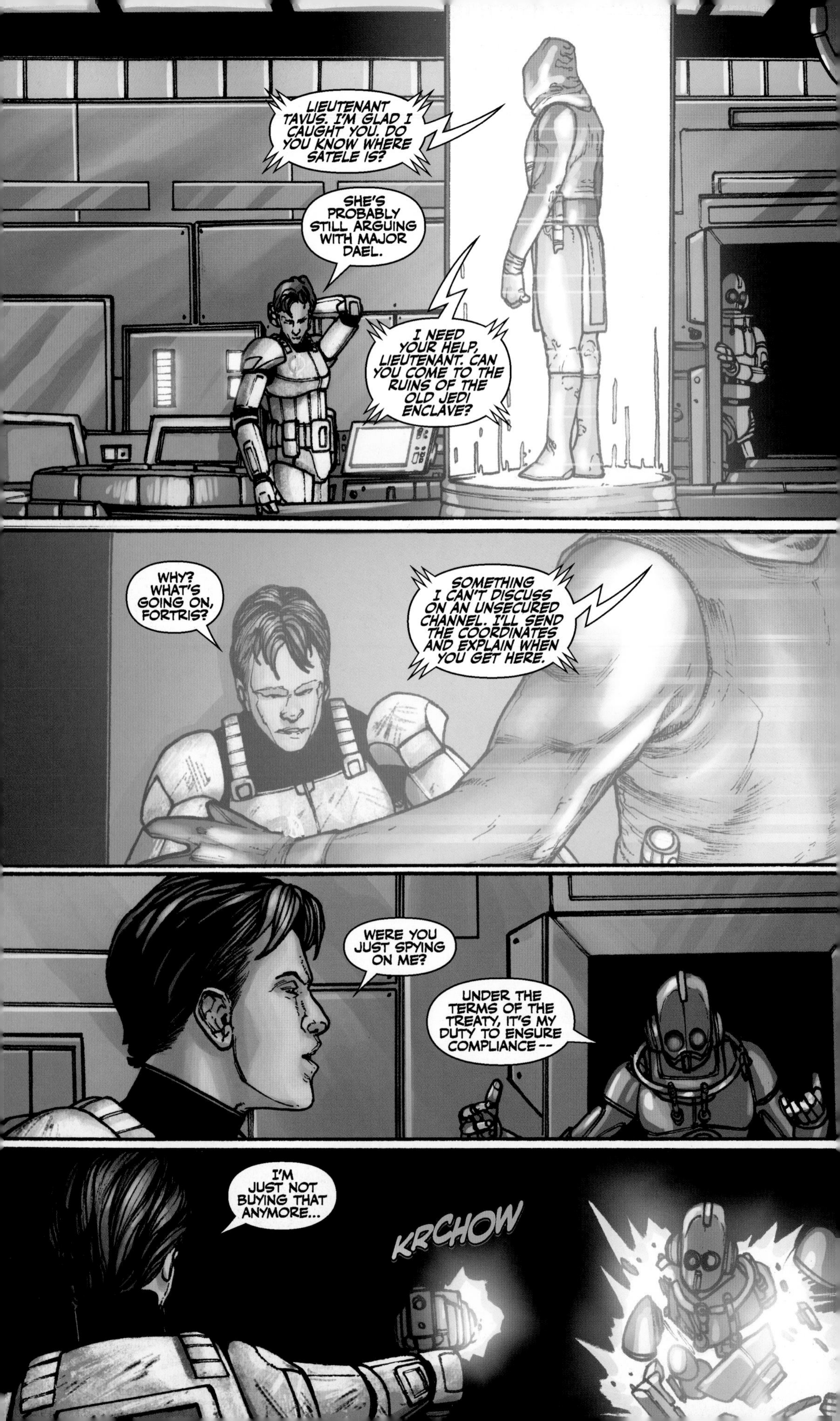
LIEUTENANT TAVUS. I'M GLAD I CAUGHT YOU. DO YOU KNOW WHERE SATELE IS?
SHE'S PROBABLY STILL ARGUING WITH MAJOR DAEL.
I NEED YOUR HELP, LIEUTENANT. CAN YOU COME TO THE RUINS OF THE OLD JEDI ENCLAVE?
WHY? WHAT'S GOING ON, FORTRIS?
SOMETHING I CAN'T DISCUSS ON AN UNSECURED CHANNEL. I'LL SEND THE COORDINATES AND EXPLAIN WHEN YOU GET HERE.
WERE YOU JUST SPYING ON ME?
UNDER THE TERMS OF THE TREATY, IT'S MY DUTY TO ENSURE COMPLIANCE --
I'M JUST NOT BUYING THAT ANYMORE...
KRCHOW

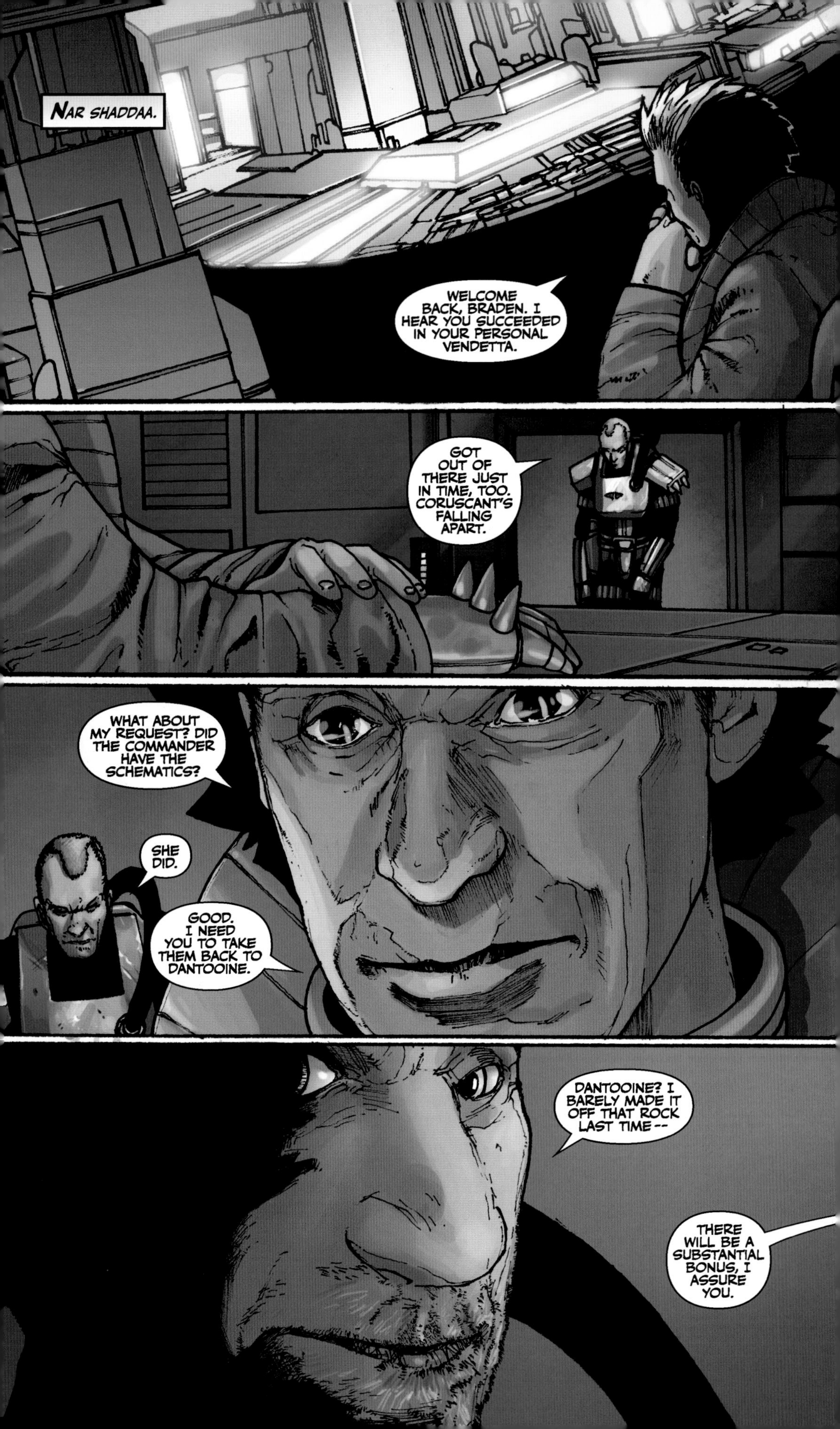
NAR SHADDAA.
WELCOME BACK, BRADEN. I HEAR YOU SUCCEEDED IN YOUR PERSONAL VENDETTA.
GOT OUT OF THERE JUST IN TIME, TOO. CORUSCANT'S FALLING APART.
WHAT ABOUT MY REQUEST? DID THE COMMANDER HAVE THE SCHEMATICS?
SHE DID.
GOOD. I NEED YOU TO TAKE THEM BACK TO DANTOOINE.
DANTOOINE? I BARELY MADE IT OFF THAT ROCK LAST TIME --
THERE WILL BE A SUBSTANTIAL BONUS, I ASSURE YOU.

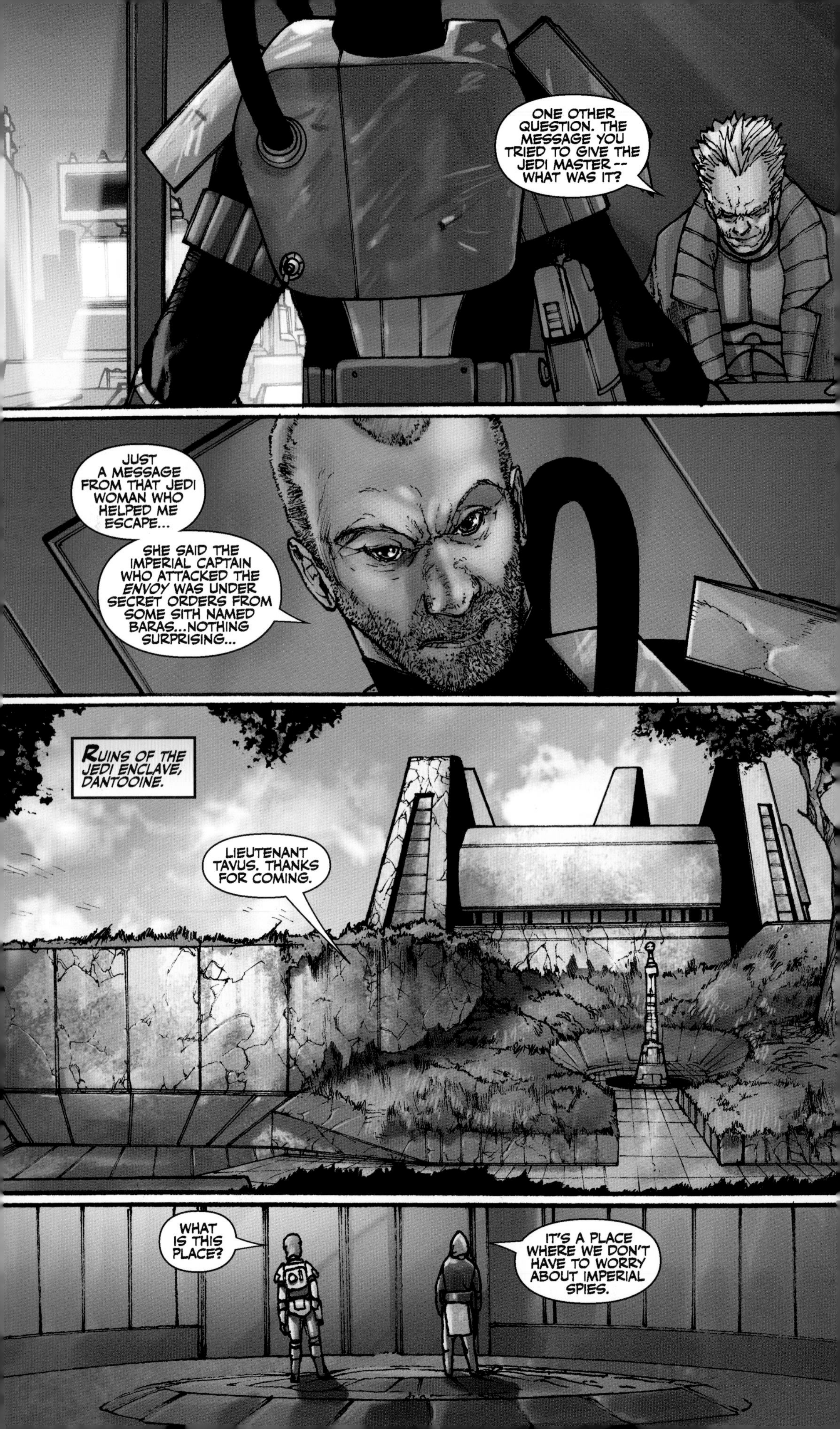
ONE OTHER QUESTION. THE MESSAGE YOU TRIED TO GIVE THE JEDI MASTER -- WHAT WAS IT?
JUST A MESSAGE FROM THAT JEDI WOMAN WHO HELPED ME ESCAPE...
SHE SAID THE IMPERIAL CAPTAIN WHO ATTACKED THE *ENVOY* WAS UNDER SECRET ORDERS FROM SOME SITH NAMED BARAS...NOTHING SURPRISING...
RUINS OF THE JEDI ENCLAVE, DANTOOINE.
LIEUTENANT TAVUS. THANKS FOR COMING.
WHAT IS THIS PLACE?
IT'S A PLACE WHERE WE DON'T HAVE TO WORRY ABOUT IMPERIAL SPIES.

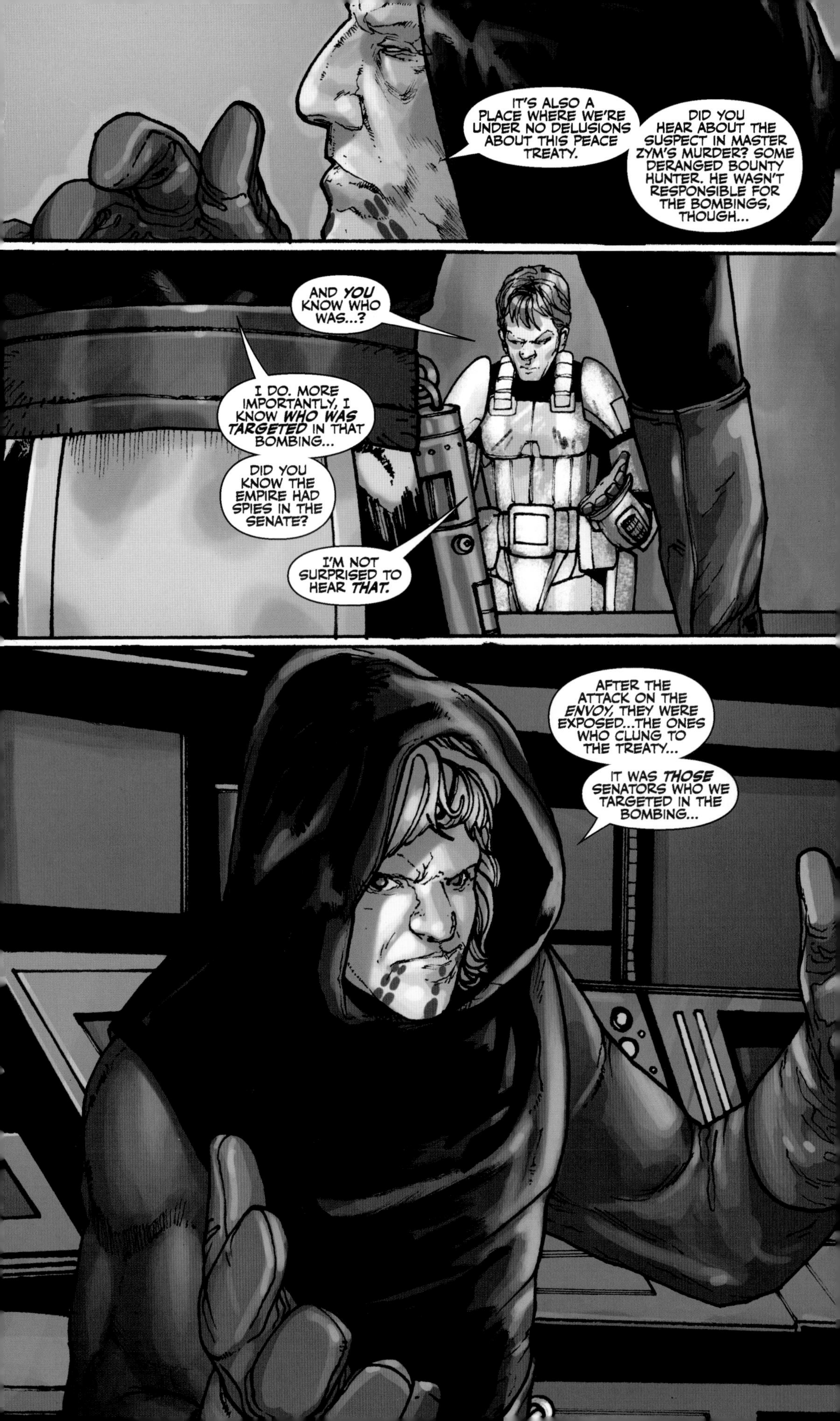
IT'S ALSO A PLACE WHERE WE'RE UNDER NO DELUSIONS ABOUT THIS PEACE TREATY.
DID YOU HEAR ABOUT THE SUSPECT IN MASTER ZYM'S MURDER? SOME DERANGED BOUNTY HUNTER. HE WASN'T RESPONSIBLE FOR THE BOMBINGS, THOUGH...
AND *YOU* KNOW WHO WAS...?
I DO. MORE IMPORTANTLY, I KNOW ***WHO WAS TARGETED*** IN THAT BOMBING...
DID YOU KNOW THE EMPIRE HAD SPIES IN THE SENATE?
I'M NOT SURPRISED TO HEAR ***THAT.***
AFTER THE ATTACK ON THE *ENVOY*, THEY WERE EXPOSED...THE ONES WHO CLUNG TO THE TREATY...
IT WAS ***THOSE*** SENATORS WHO WE TARGETED IN THE BOMBING...

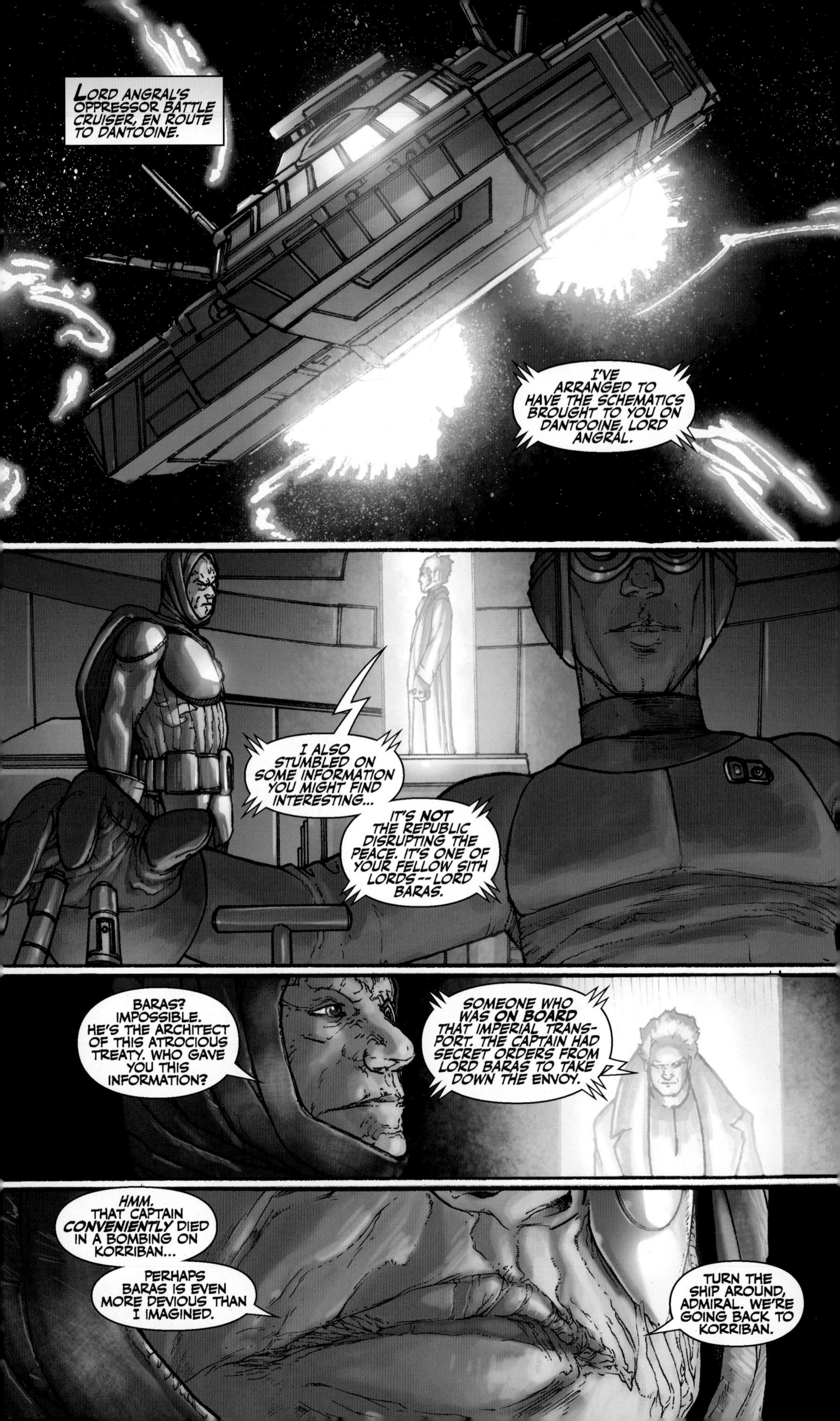
LORD ANGRAL'S OPPRESSOR BATTLE CRUISER, EN ROUTE TO DANTOOINE.
I'VE ARRANGED TO HAVE THE SCHEMATICS BROUGHT TO YOU ON DANTOOINE, LORD ANGRAL.
I ALSO STUMBLED ON SOME INFORMATION YOU MIGHT FIND INTERESTING...
IT'S NOT THE REPUBLIC DISRUPTING THE PEACE. IT'S ONE OF YOUR FELLOW SITH LORDS--LORD BARAS.
BARAS? IMPOSSIBLE. HE'S THE ARCHITECT OF THIS ATROCIOUS TREATY. WHO GAVE YOU THIS INFORMATION?
SOMEONE WHO WAS ON BOARD THAT IMPERIAL TRANSPORT. THE CAPTAIN HAD SECRET ORDERS FROM LORD BARAS TO TAKE DOWN THE ENVOY.
HMM. THAT CAPTAIN CONVENIENTLY DIED IN A BOMBING ON KORRIBAN...
PERHAPS BARAS IS EVEN MORE DEVIOUS THAN I IMAGINED.
TURN THE SHIP AROUND, ADMIRAL. WE'RE GOING BACK TO KORRIBAN.

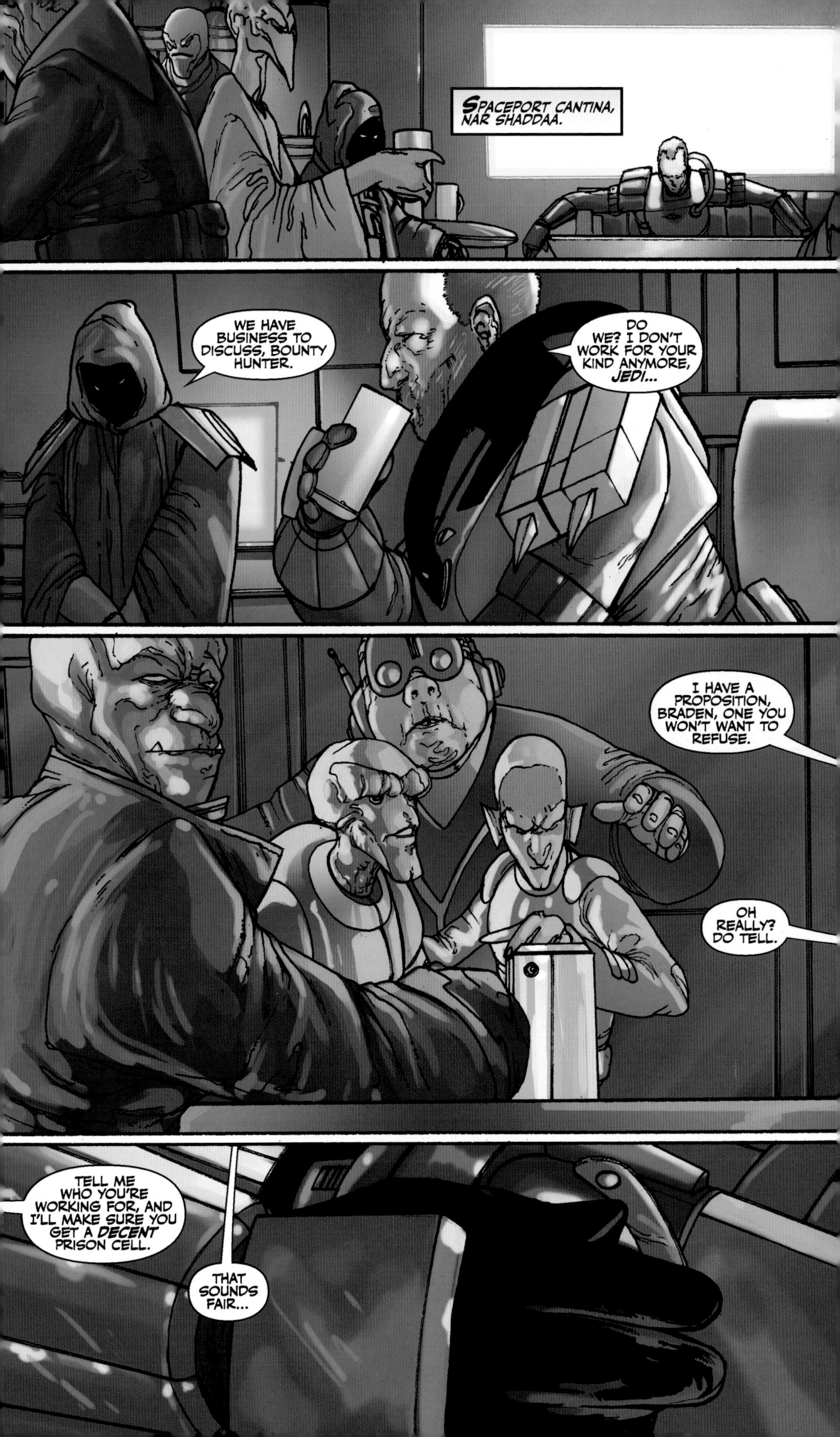
SPACEPORT CANTINA, NAR SHADDAA.
WE HAVE BUSINESS TO DISCUSS, BOUNTY HUNTER.
DO WE? I DON'T WORK FOR YOUR KIND ANYMORE, *JEDI*...
I HAVE A PROPOSITION, BRADEN, ONE YOU WON'T WANT TO REFUSE.
OH REALLY? DO TELL.
TELL ME WHO YOU'RE WORKING FOR, AND I'LL MAKE SURE YOU GET A *DECENT* PRISON CELL.
THAT SOUNDS FAIR...

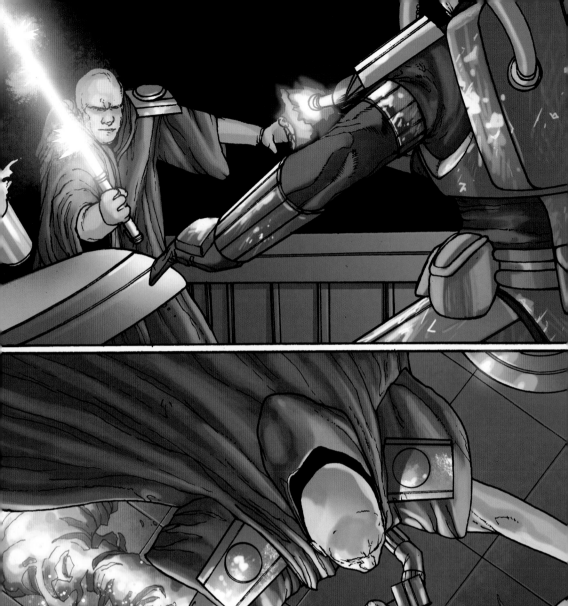

TIME TO RECONSIDER.

I HAD NOTHING TO DO WITH THE BOMBING.

IF YOU WANT THE GUY WHO'S BREAKING UP THE PEACE TREATY, I CAN HELP YOU.

BUT WE'LL HAVE TO GO TO DANTOOINE...

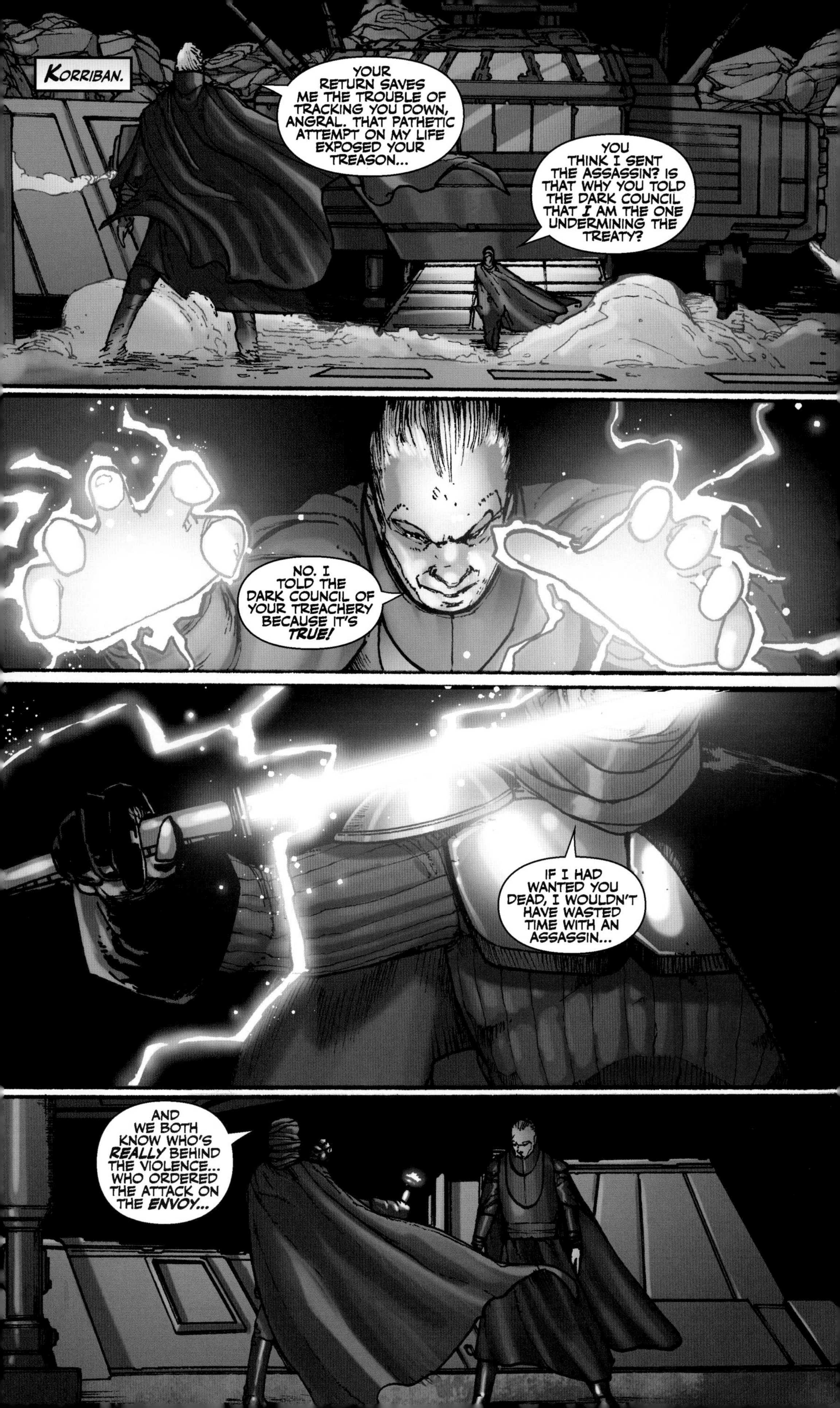
KORRIBAN.
YOUR RETURN SAVES ME THE TROUBLE OF TRACKING YOU DOWN, ANGRAL. THAT PATHETIC ATTEMPT ON MY LIFE EXPOSED YOUR TREASON...
YOU THINK I SENT THE ASSASSIN? IS THAT WHY YOU TOLD THE DARK COUNCIL THAT I AM THE ONE UNDERMINING THE TREATY?
NO. I TOLD THE DARK COUNCIL OF YOUR TREACHERY BECAUSE IT'S TRUE!
IF I HAD WANTED YOU DEAD, I WOULDN'T HAVE WASTED TIME WITH AN ASSASSIN...
AND WE BOTH KNOW WHO'S REALLY BEHIND THE VIOLENCE... WHO ORDERED THE ATTACK ON THE ENVOY...

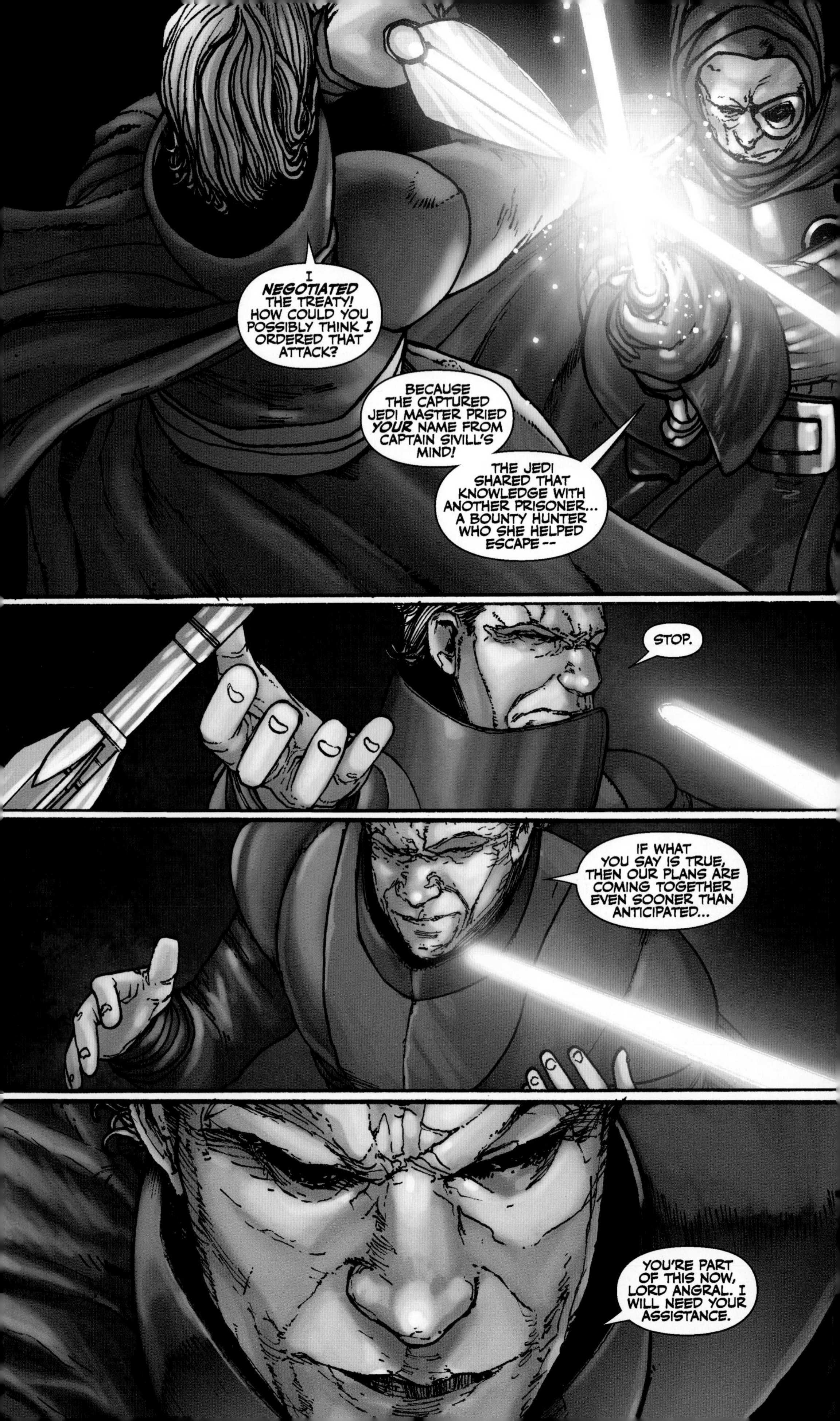
I NEGOTIATED THE TREATY! HOW COULD YOU POSSIBLY THINK I ORDERED THAT ATTACK?
BECAUSE THE CAPTURED JEDI MASTER PRIED YOUR NAME FROM CAPTAIN SIVILL'S MIND!
THE JEDI SHARED THAT KNOWLEDGE WITH ANOTHER PRISONER... A BOUNTY HUNTER WHO SHE HELPED ESCAPE --
STOP.
IF WHAT YOU SAY IS TRUE, THEN OUR PLANS ARE COMING TOGETHER EVEN SOONER THAN ANTICIPATED...
YOU'RE PART OF THIS NOW, LORD ANGRAL. I WILL NEED YOUR ASSISTANCE.

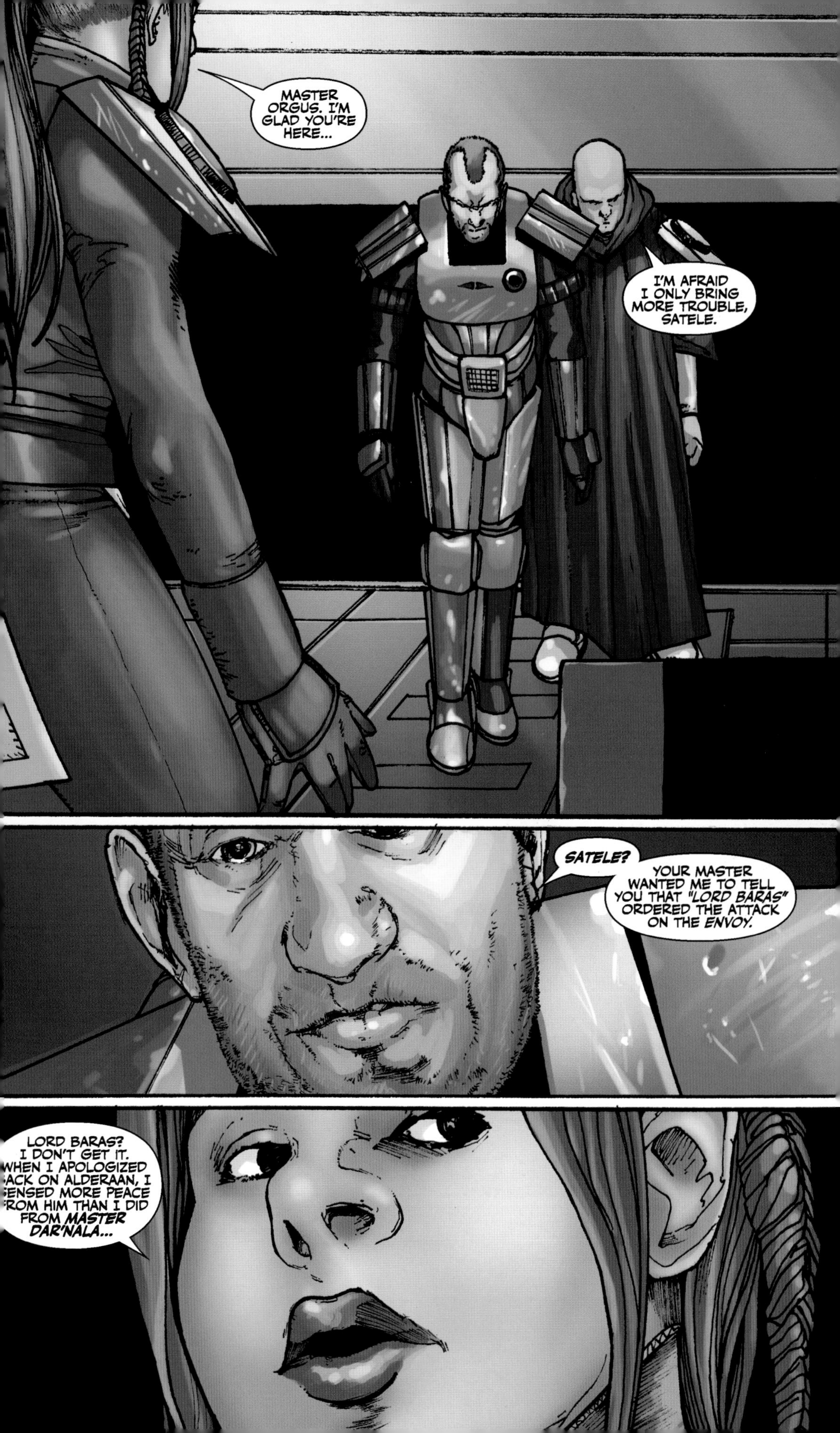
MASTER ORGUS. I'M GLAD YOU'RE HERE...
I'M AFRAID I ONLY BRING MORE TROUBLE, SATELE.
SATELE?
YOUR MASTER WANTED ME TO TELL YOU THAT "LORD BARAS" ORDERED THE ATTACK ON THE ENVOY.
LORD BARAS? I DON'T GET IT. WHEN I APOLOGIZED BACK ON ALDERAAN, I SENSED MORE PEACE FROM HIM THAN I DID FROM MASTER DAR'NALA...

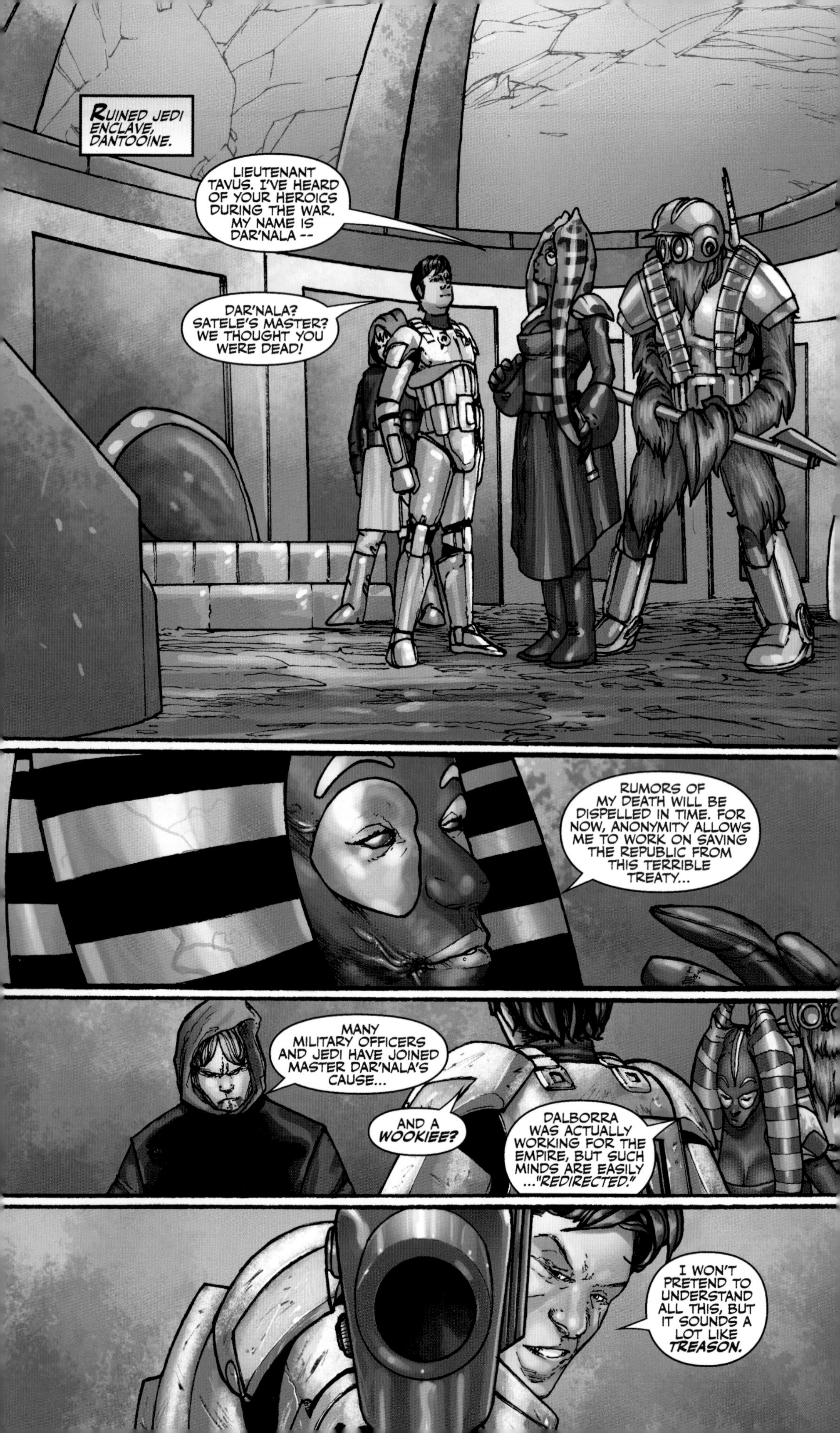
RUINED JEDI ENCLAVE, DANTOOINE.
LIEUTENANT TAVUS. I'VE HEARD OF YOUR HEROICS DURING THE WAR. MY NAME IS DAR'NALA --
DAR'NALA? SATELE'S MASTER? WE THOUGHT YOU WERE DEAD!
RUMORS OF MY DEATH WILL BE DISPELLED IN TIME. FOR NOW, ANONYMITY ALLOWS ME TO WORK ON SAVING THE REPUBLIC FROM THIS TERRIBLE TREATY...
MANY MILITARY OFFICERS AND JEDI HAVE JOINED MASTER DAR'NALA'S CAUSE...
AND A *WOOKIEE?*
DALBORRA WAS ACTUALLY WORKING FOR THE EMPIRE, BUT SUCH MINDS ARE EASILY ..."REDIRECTED."
I WON'T PRETEND TO UNDERSTAND ALL THIS, BUT IT SOUNDS A LOT LIKE *TREASON.*

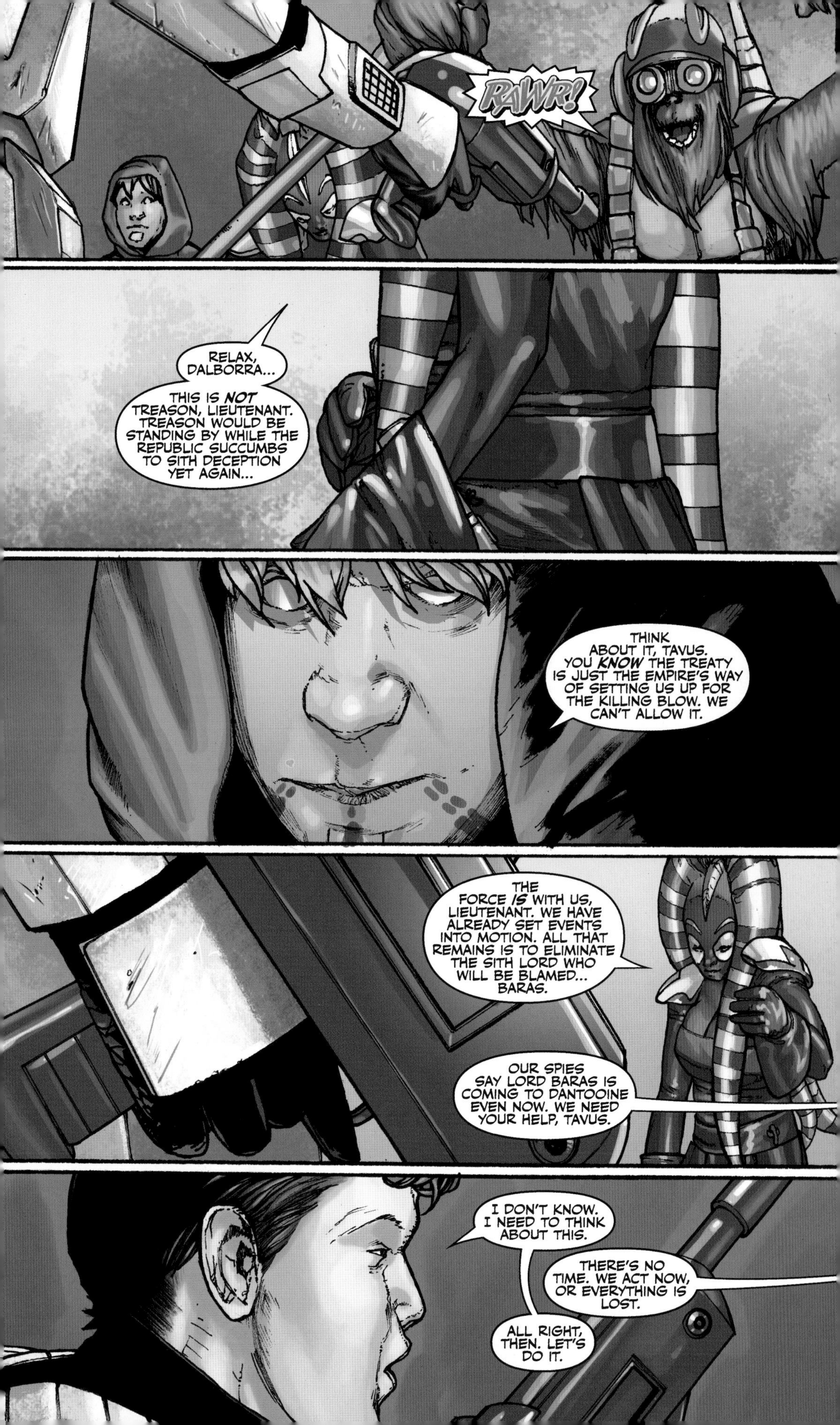
RAWR!
RELAX, DALBORRA...
THIS IS NOT TREASON, LIEUTENANT. TREASON WOULD BE STANDING BY WHILE THE REPUBLIC SUCCUMBS TO SITH DECEPTION YET AGAIN...
THINK ABOUT IT, TAVUS. YOU KNOW THE TREATY IS JUST THE EMPIRE'S WAY OF SETTING US UP FOR THE KILLING BLOW. WE CAN'T ALLOW IT.
THE FORCE IS WITH US, LIEUTENANT. WE HAVE ALREADY SET EVENTS INTO MOTION. ALL THAT REMAINS IS TO ELIMINATE THE SITH LORD WHO WILL BE BLAMED... BARAS.
OUR SPIES SAY LORD BARAS IS COMING TO DANTOOINE EVEN NOW. WE NEED YOUR HELP, TAVUS.
I DON'T KNOW. I NEED TO THINK ABOUT THIS.
THERE'S NO TIME. WE ACT NOW, OR EVERYTHING IS LOST.
ALL RIGHT, THEN. LET'S DO IT.

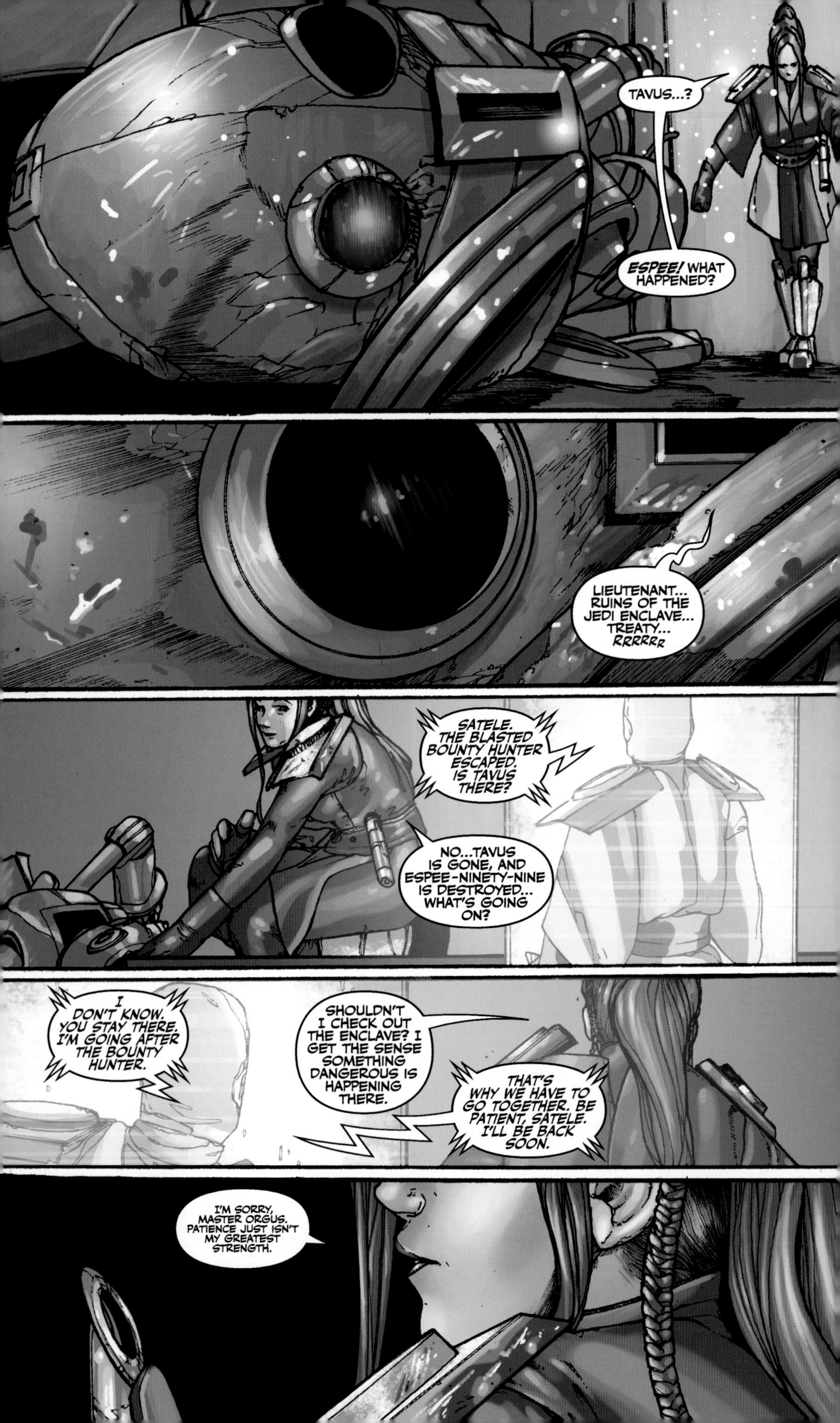

TAVUS...?
ESPEE! WHAT HAPPENED?
LIEUTENANT... RUINS OF THE JEDI ENCLAVE... TREATY... RRRRRR
SATELE. THE BLASTED BOUNTY HUNTER ESCAPED. IS TAVUS THERE?
NO...TAVUS IS GONE, AND ESPEE-NINETY-NINE IS DESTROYED... WHAT'S GOING ON?
I DON'T KNOW. YOU STAY THERE. I'M GOING AFTER THE BOUNTY HUNTER.
SHOULDN'T I CHECK OUT THE ENCLAVE? I GET THE SENSE SOMETHING DANGEROUS IS HAPPENING THERE.
THAT'S WHY WE HAVE TO GO TOGETHER. BE PATIENT, SATELE. I'LL BE BACK SOON.
I'M SORRY, MASTER ORGUS. PATIENCE JUST ISN'T MY GREATEST STRENGTH.

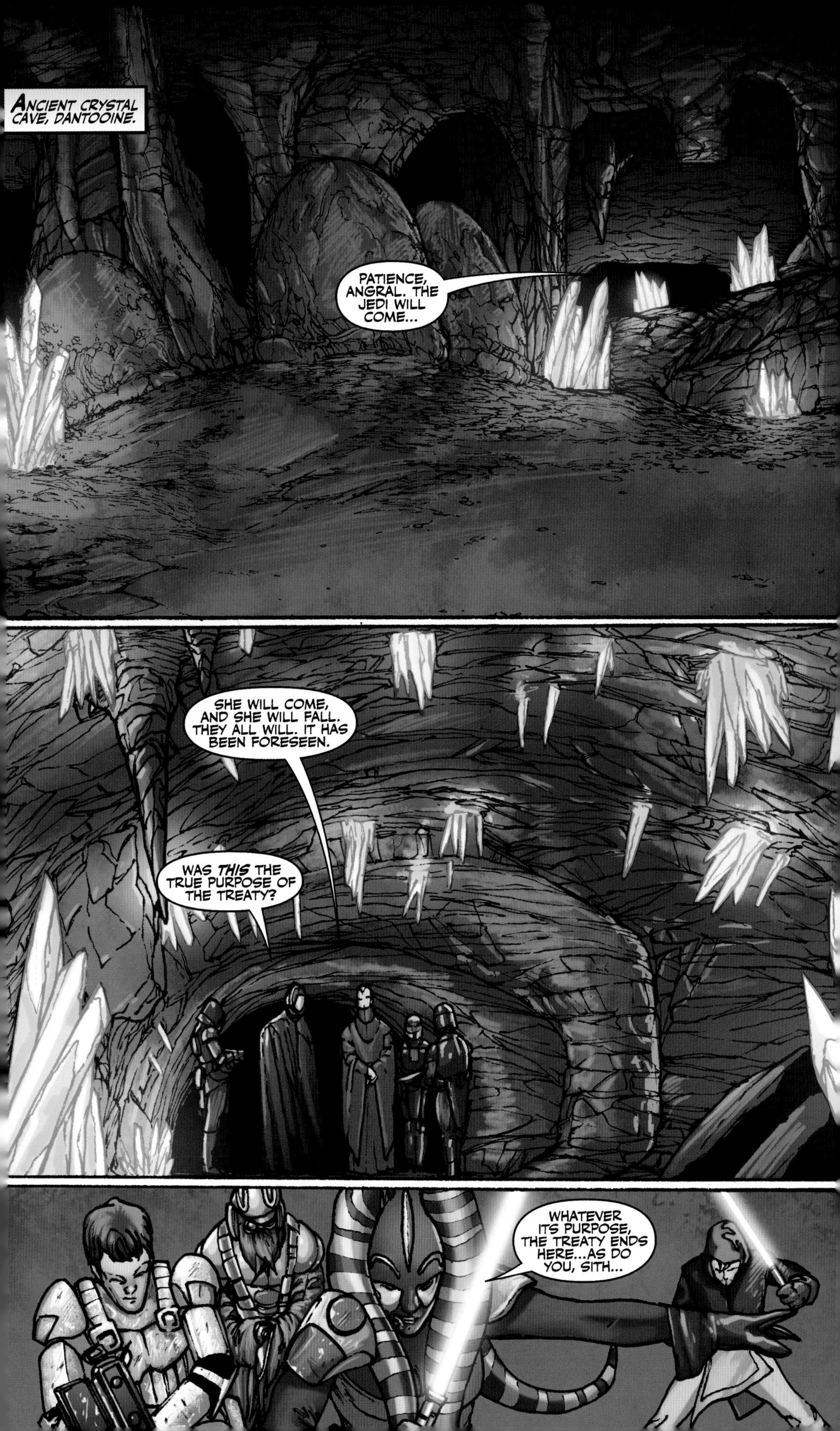
ANCIENT CRYSTAL CAVE, DANTOOINE.
PATIENCE, ANGRAL. THE JEDI WILL COME...
SHE WILL COME, AND SHE WILL FALL. THEY ALL WILL. IT HAS BEEN FORESEEN.
WAS *THIS* THE TRUE PURPOSE OF THE TREATY?
WHATEVER ITS PURPOSE, THE TREATY ENDS HERE...AS DO YOU, SITH...

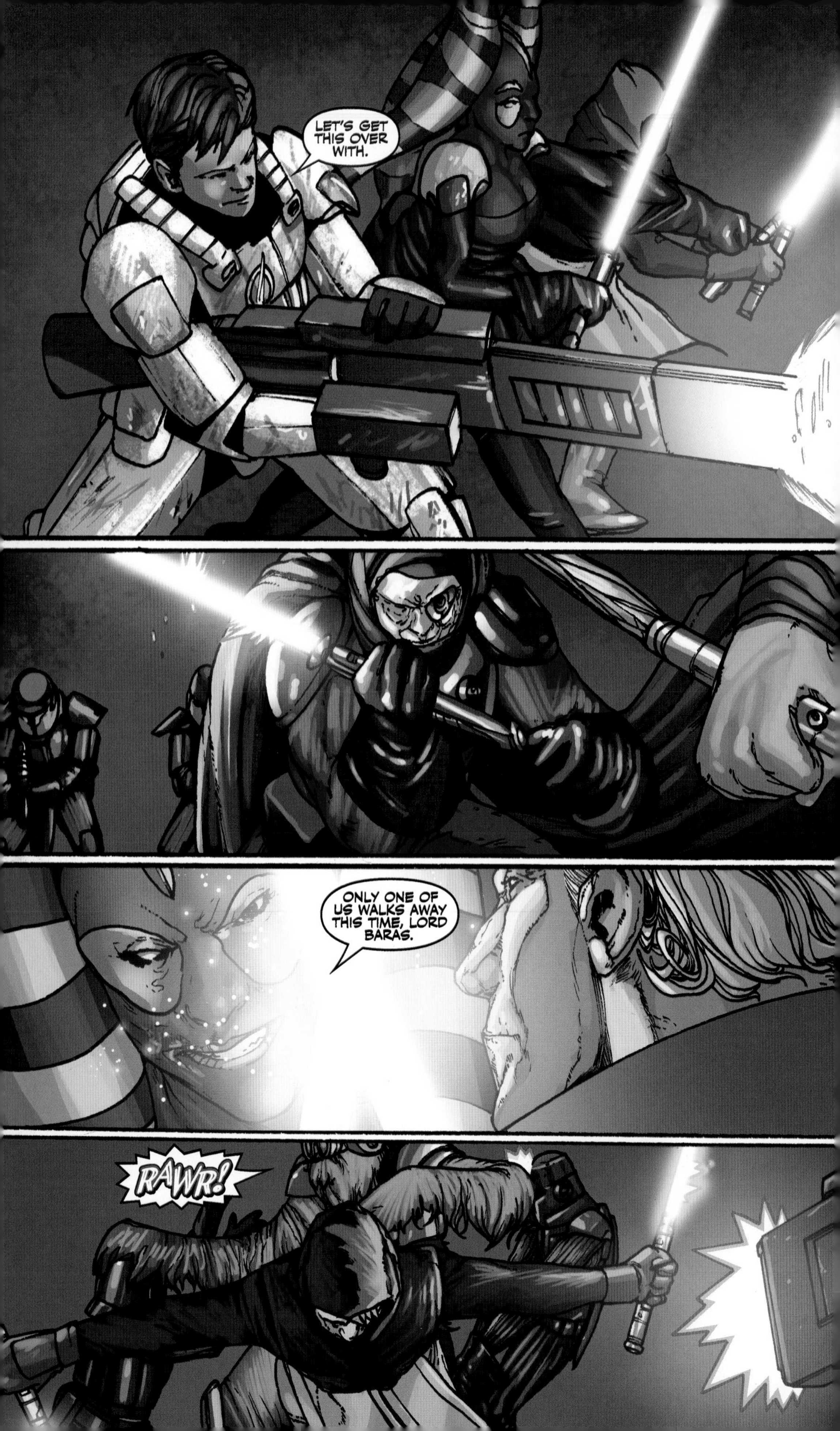
LET'S GET THIS OVER WITH.
ONLY ONE OF US WALKS AWAY THIS TIME, LORD BARAS.
RAWR!

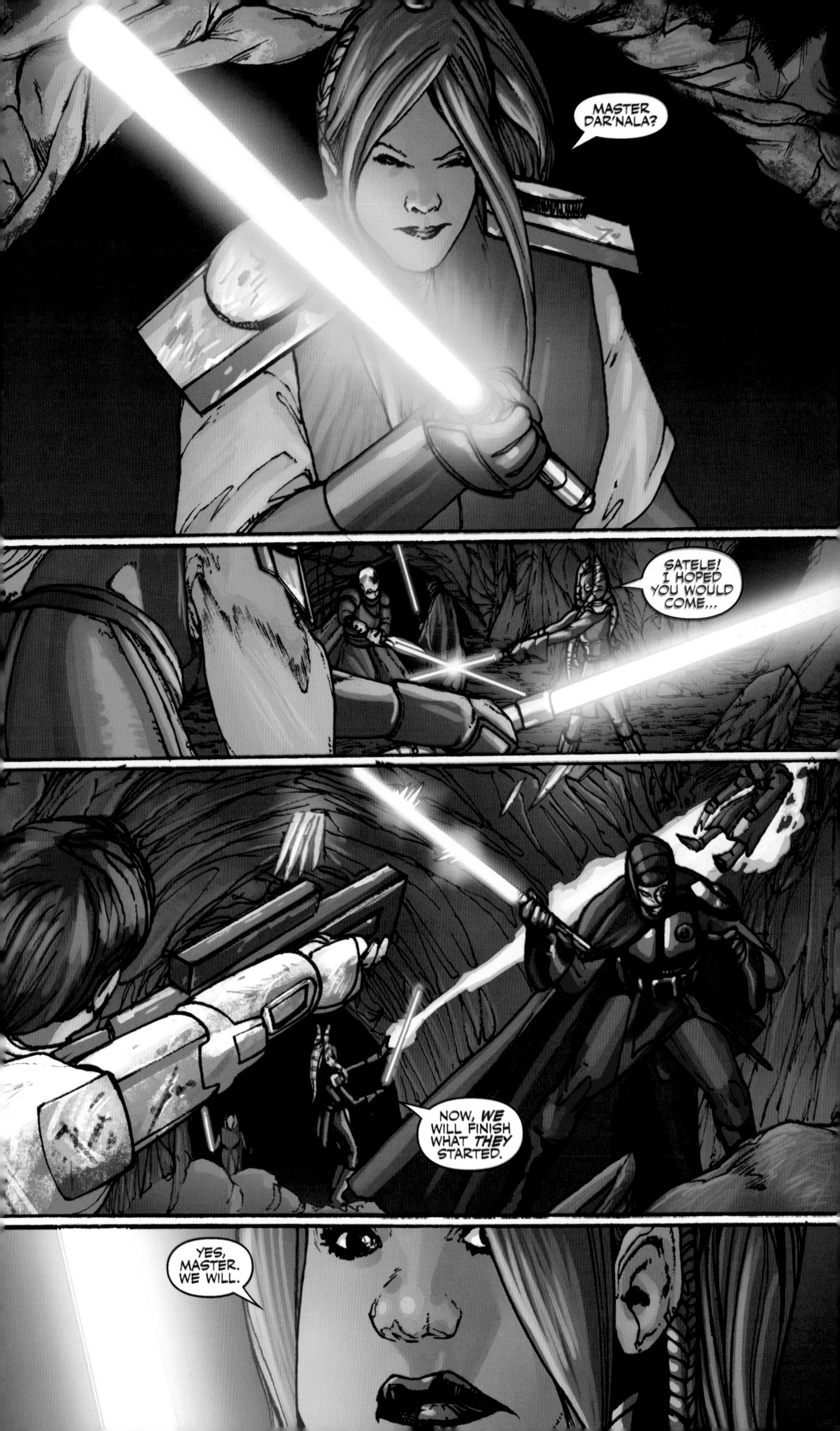
MASTER DAR'NALA?
SATELE! I HOPED YOU WOULD COME...
NOW, *WE* WILL FINISH WHAT *THEY* STARTED.
YES, MASTER. WE WILL.

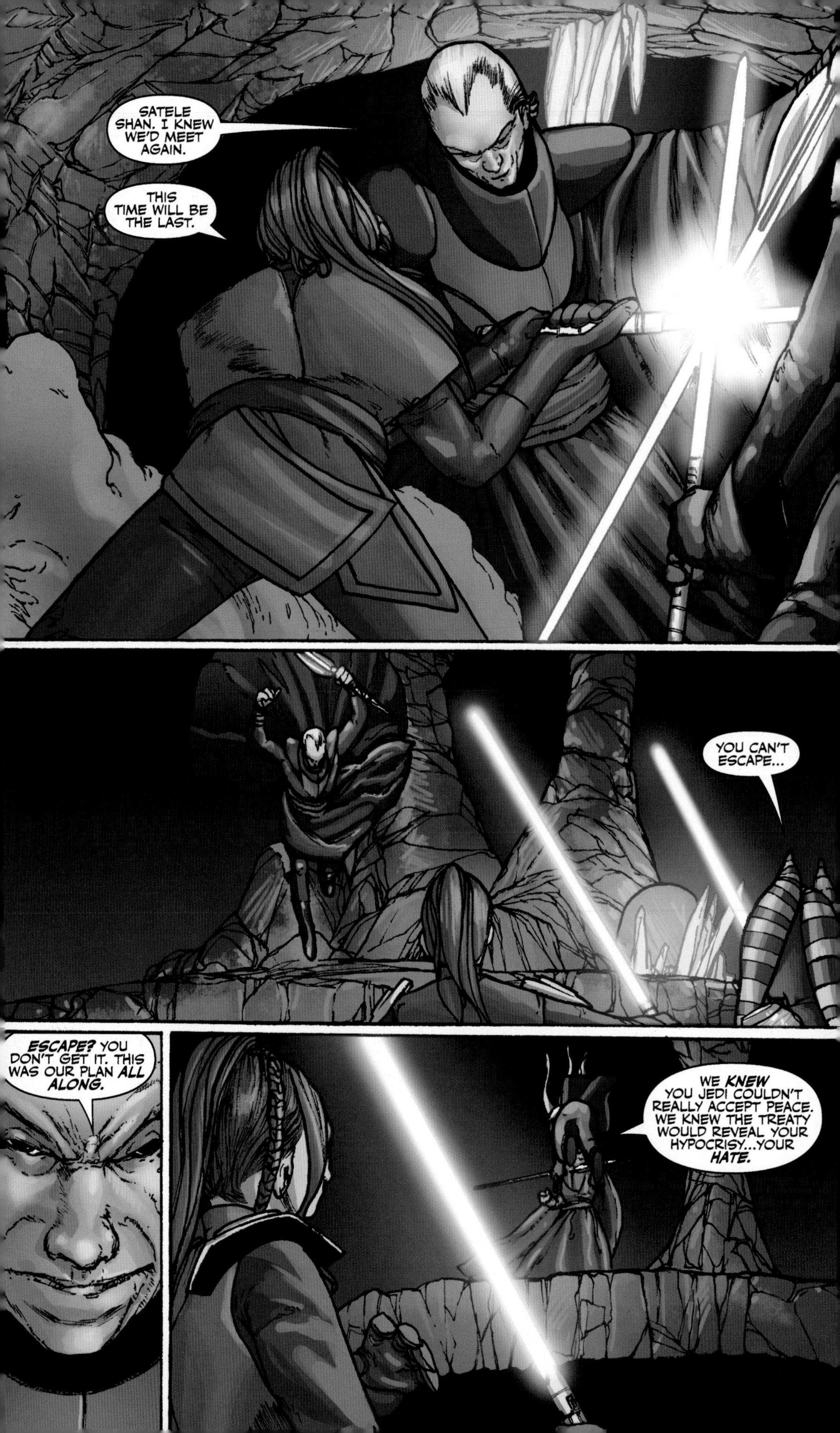
SATELE SHAN. I KNEW WE'D MEET AGAIN.
THIS TIME WILL BE THE LAST.
YOU CAN'T ESCAPE...
ESCAPE? YOU DON'T GET IT. THIS WAS OUR PLAN *ALL ALONG*.
WE *KNEW* YOU JEDI COULDN'T REALLY ACCEPT PEACE. WE KNEW THE TREATY WOULD REVEAL YOUR HYPOCRISY...YOUR *HATE*.

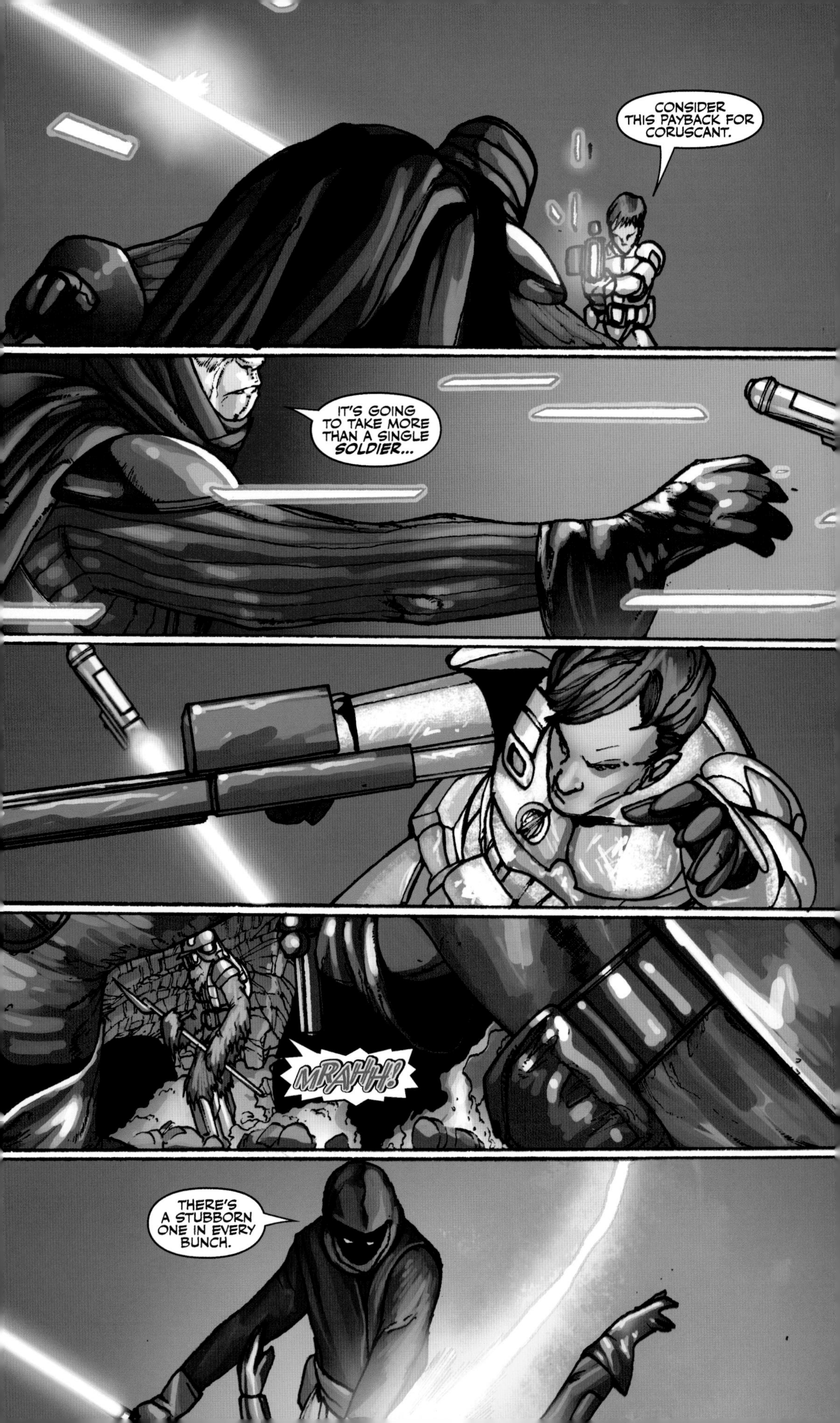
CONSIDER THIS PAYBACK FOR CORUSCANT.
IT'S GOING TO TAKE MORE THAN A SINGLE *SOLDIER*...
MRAHH!
THERE'S A STUBBORN ONE IN EVERY BUNCH.

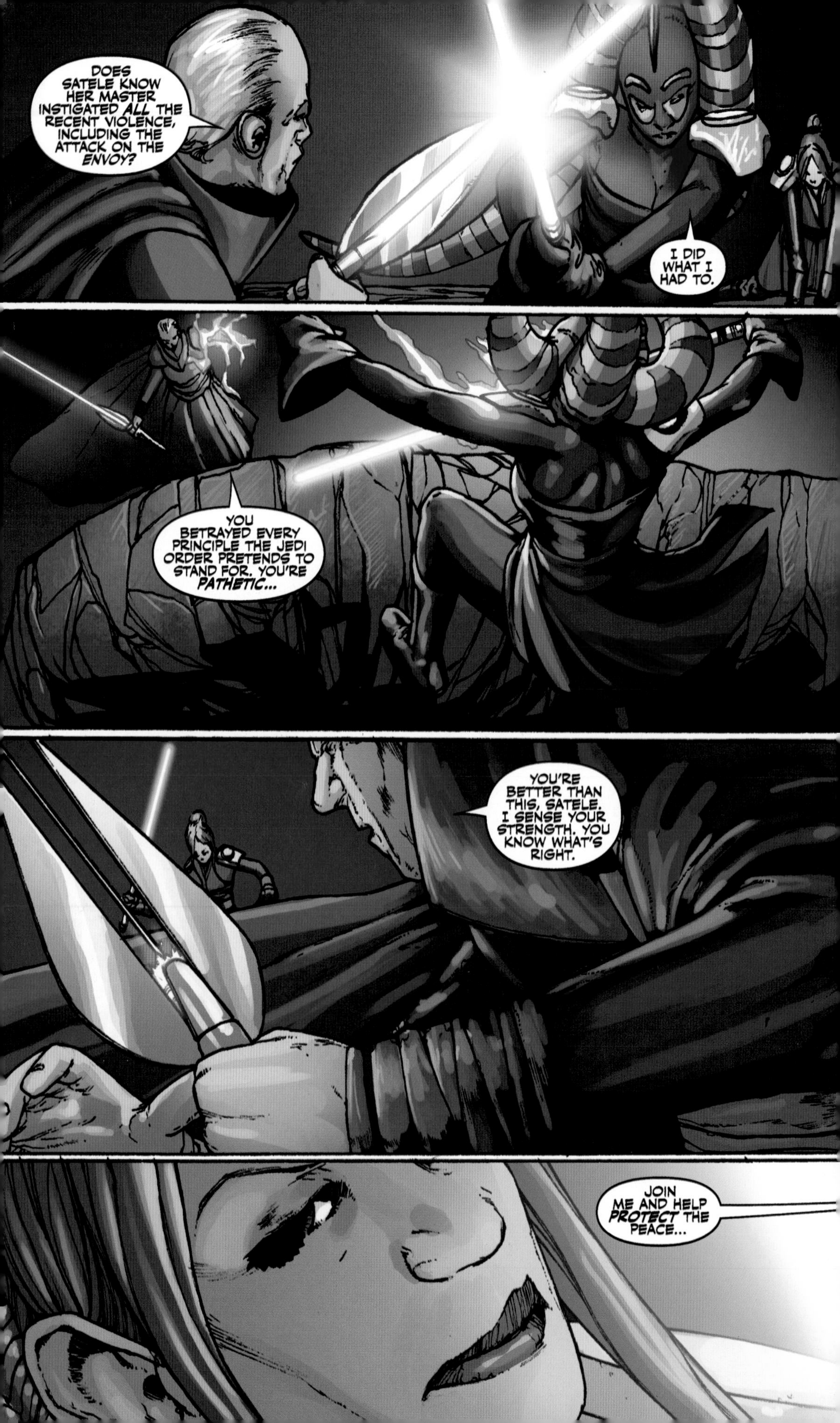
DOES SATELE KNOW HER MASTER INSTIGATED ALL THE RECENT VIOLENCE, INCLUDING THE ATTACK ON THE ENVOY?
I DID WHAT I HAD TO.
YOU BETRAYED EVERY PRINCIPLE THE JEDI ORDER PRETENDS TO STAND FOR. YOU'RE PATHETIC...
YOU'RE BETTER THAN THIS, SATELE. I SENSE YOUR STRENGTH. YOU KNOW WHAT'S RIGHT.
JOIN ME AND HELP PROTECT THE PEACE...

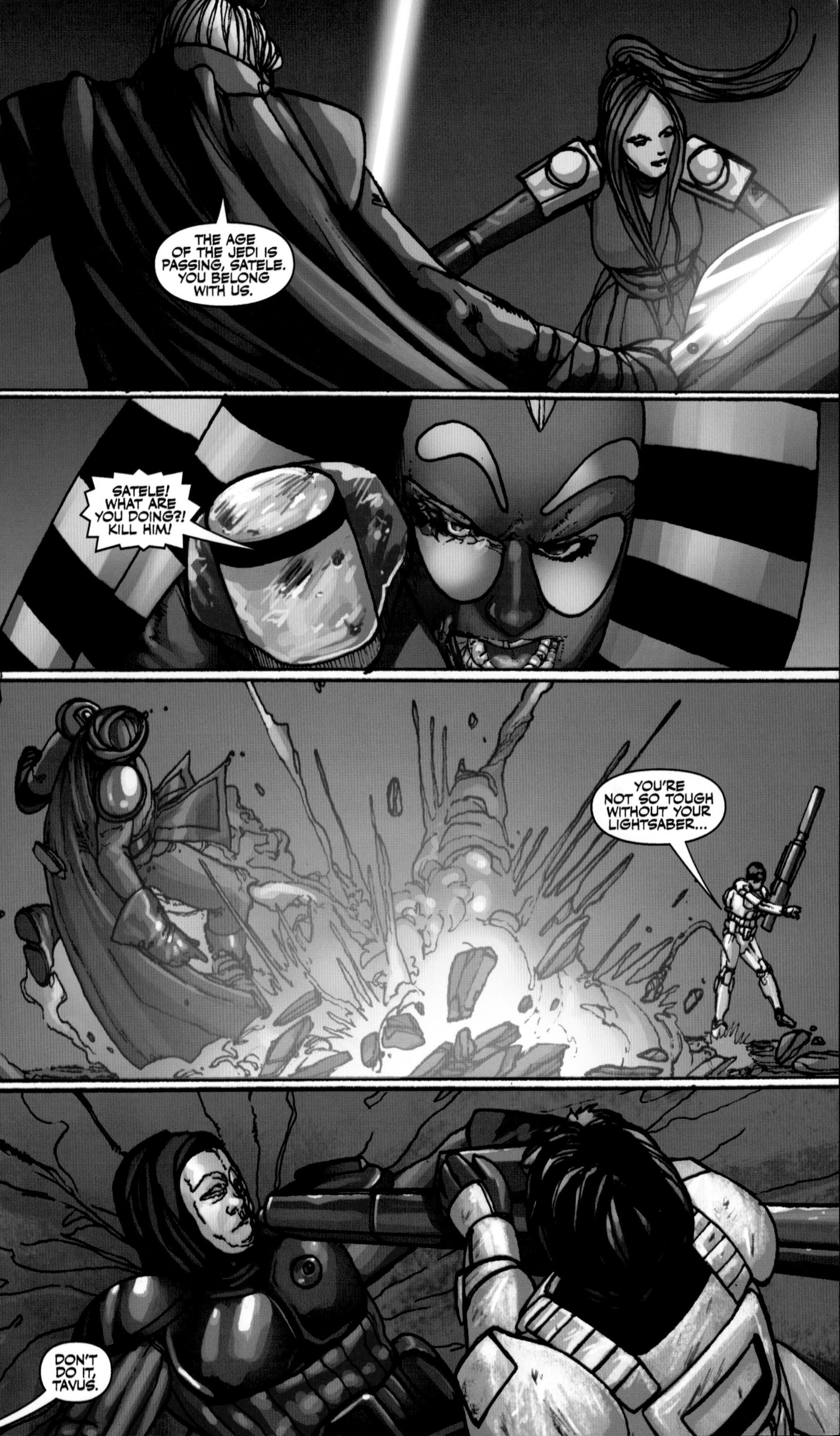
THE AGE OF THE JEDI IS PASSING, SATELE. YOU BELONG WITH US.
SATELE! WHAT ARE YOU DOING?! KILL HIM!
YOU'RE NOT SO TOUGH WITHOUT YOUR LIGHTSABER...
DON'T DO IT, TAVUS.

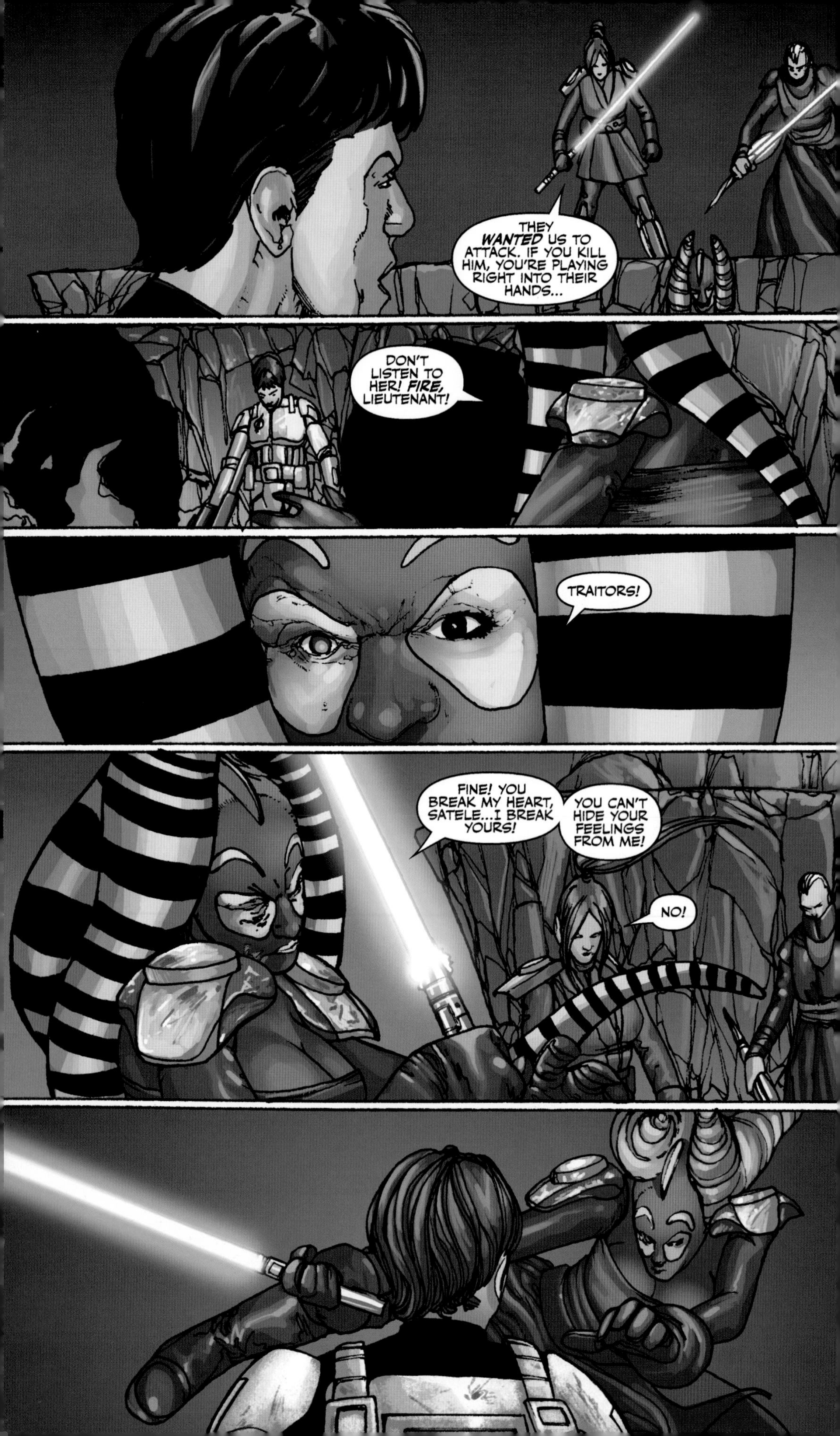
THEY *WANTED* US TO ATTACK. IF YOU KILL HIM, YOU'RE PLAYING RIGHT INTO THEIR HANDS...
DON'T LISTEN TO HER! *FIRE,* LIEUTENANT!
TRAITORS!
FINE! YOU BREAK MY HEART, SATELE...I BREAK YOURS!
YOU CAN'T HIDE YOUR FEELINGS FROM ME!
NO!

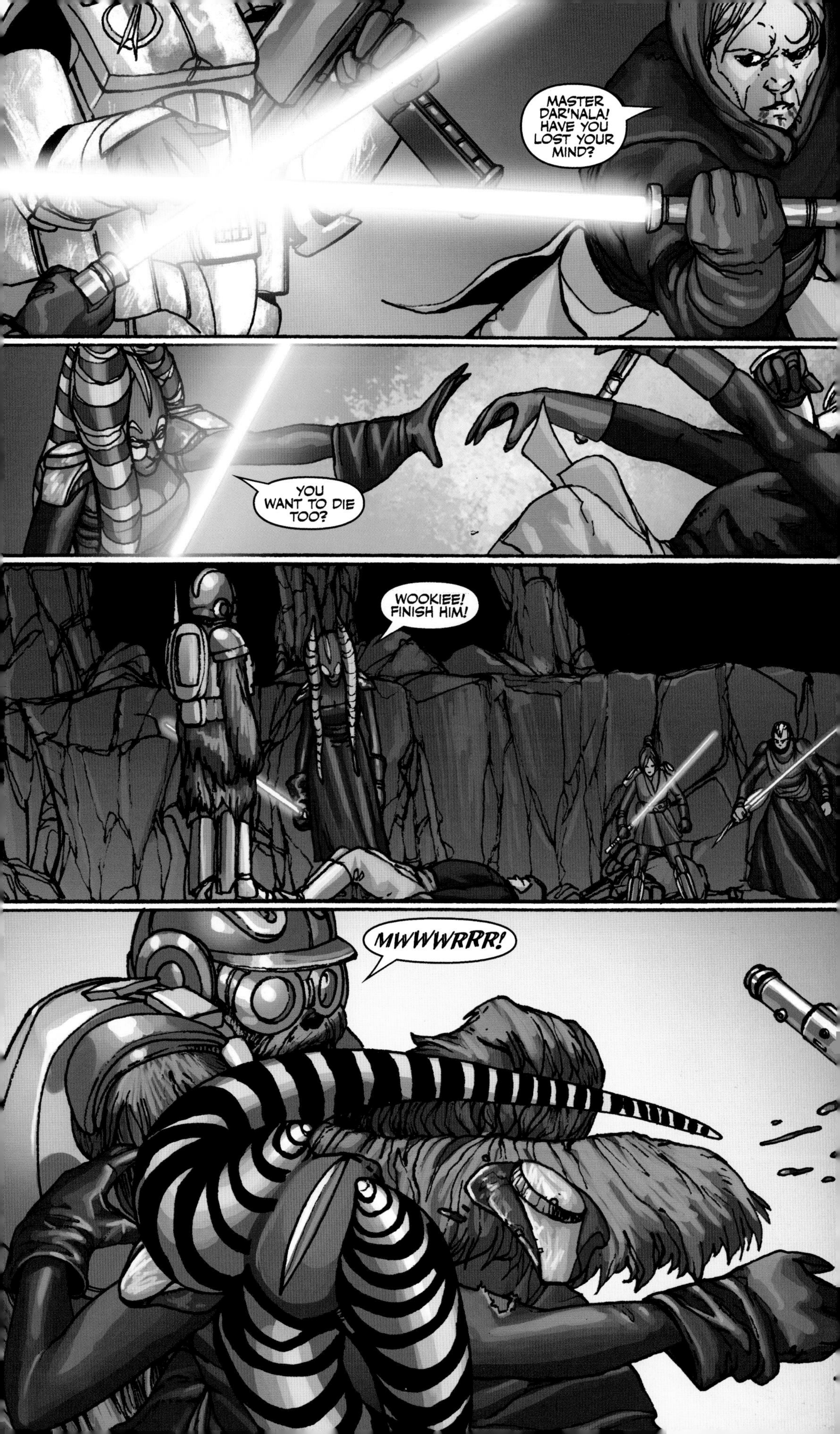
MASTER DAR'NALA! HAVE YOU LOST YOUR MIND?
YOU WANT TO DIE TOO?
WOOKIEE! FINISH HIM!
MWWWRRR!

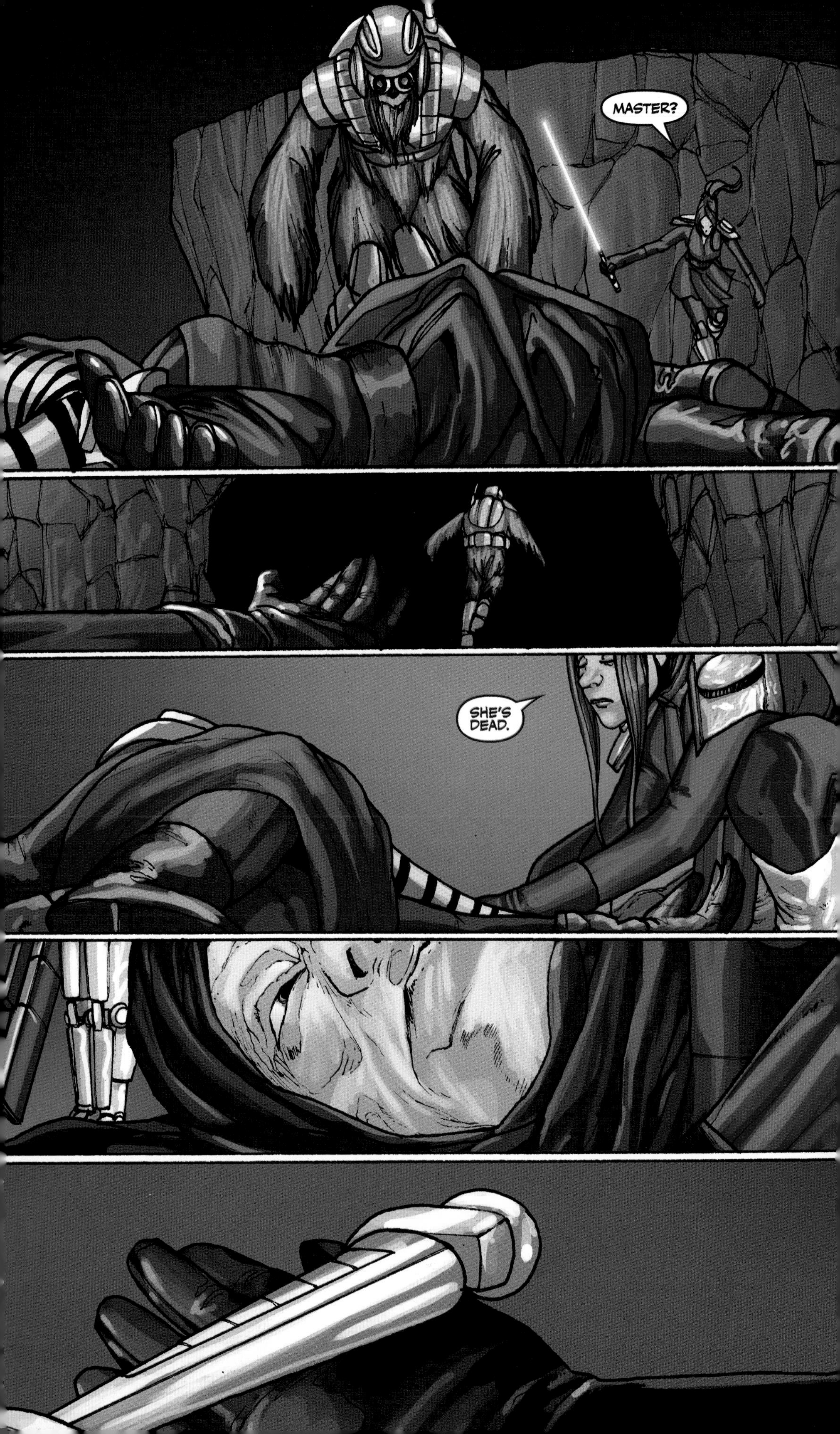
MASTER?
SHE'S DEAD.

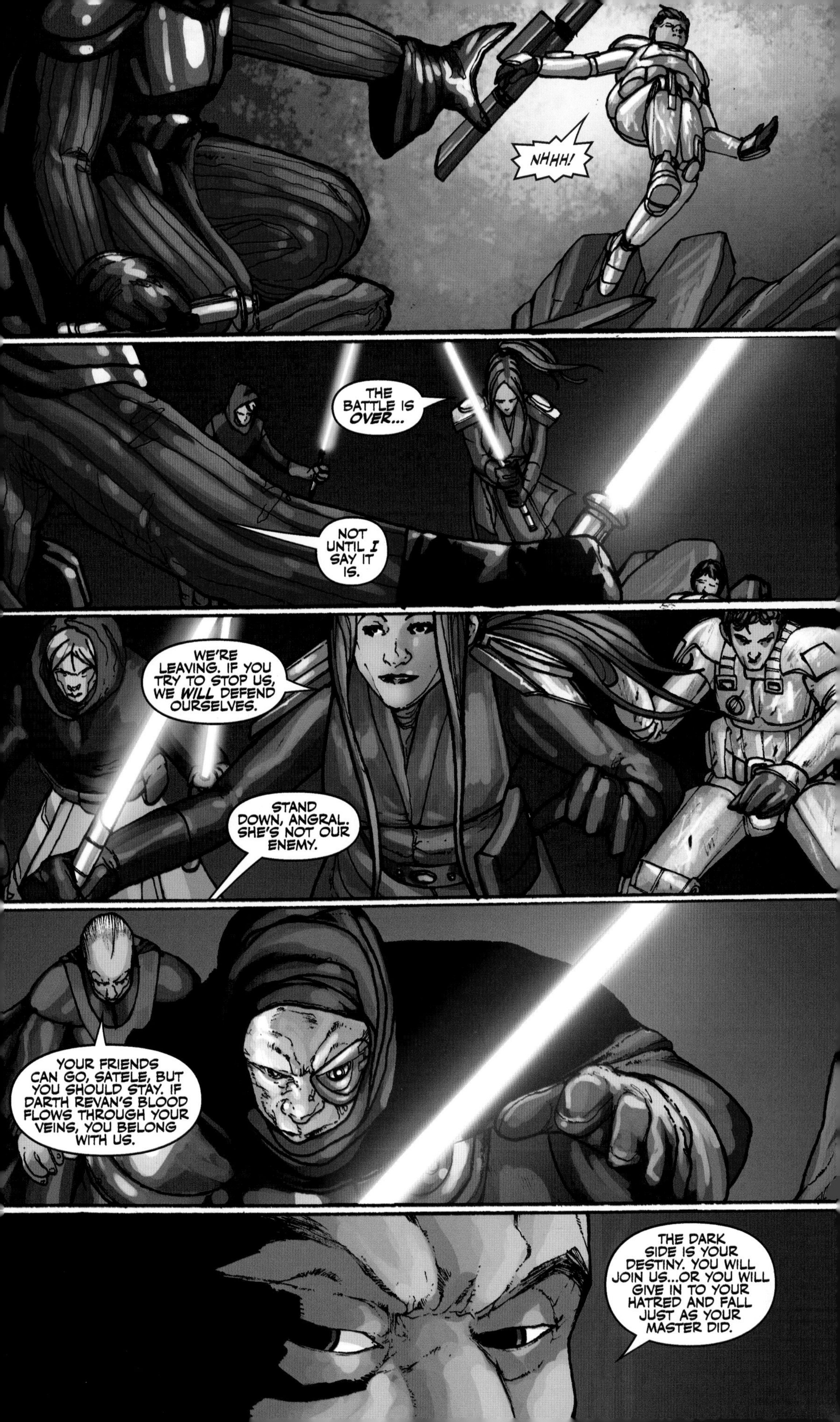
NHHH!
THE BATTLE IS *OVER*...
NOT UNTIL *I* SAY IT IS.
WE'RE LEAVING. IF YOU TRY TO STOP US, WE *WILL* DEFEND OURSELVES.
STAND DOWN, ANGRAL. SHE'S NOT OUR ENEMY.
YOUR FRIENDS CAN GO, SATELE, BUT YOU SHOULD STAY. IF DARTH REVAN'S BLOOD FLOWS THROUGH YOUR VEINS, YOU BELONG WITH US.
THE DARK SIDE IS YOUR DESTINY. YOU WILL JOIN US...OR YOU WILL GIVE IN TO YOUR HATRED AND FALL JUST AS YOUR MASTER DID.

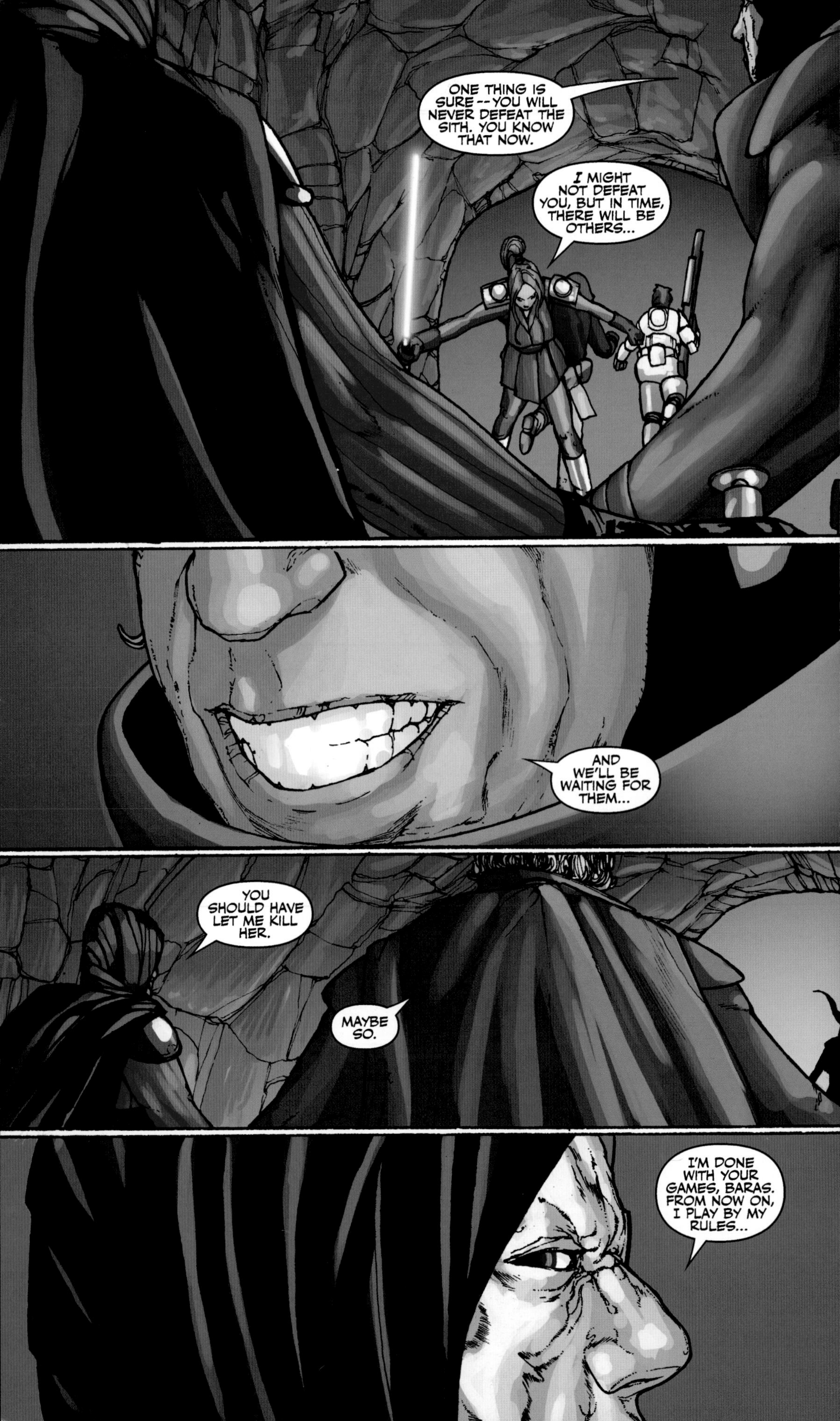
ONE THING IS SURE--YOU WILL NEVER DEFEAT THE SITH. YOU KNOW THAT NOW.
I MIGHT NOT DEFEAT YOU, BUT IN TIME, THERE WILL BE OTHERS...
AND WE'LL BE WAITING FOR THEM...
YOU SHOULD HAVE LET ME KILL HER.
MAYBE SO.
I'M DONE WITH YOUR GAMES, BARAS. FROM NOW ON, I PLAY BY MY RULES...

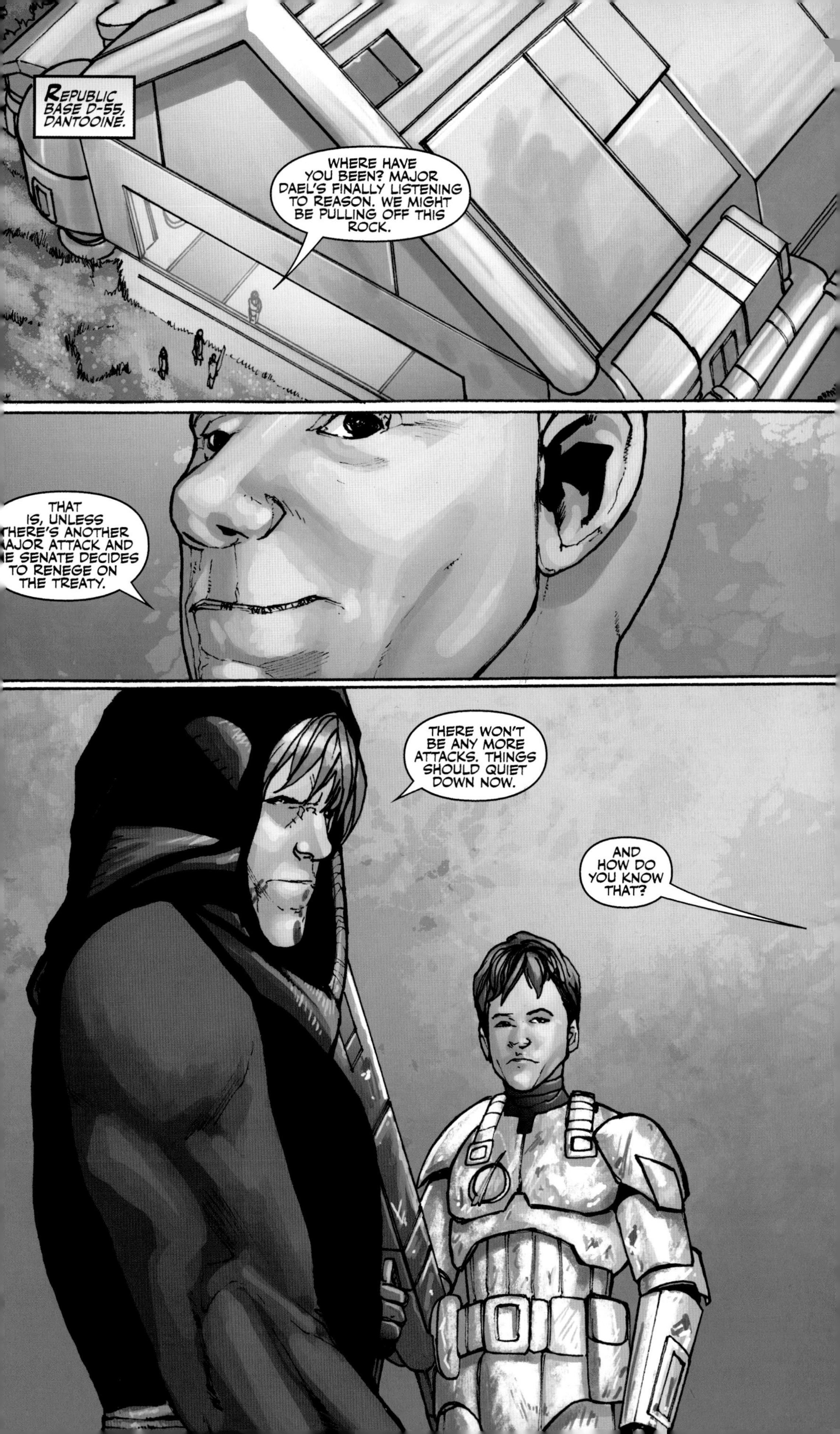
REPUBLIC BASE D-55, DANTOOINE.
WHERE HAVE YOU BEEN? MAJOR DAEL'S FINALLY LISTENING TO REASON. WE MIGHT BE PULLING OFF THIS ROCK.
THAT IS, UNLESS THERE'S ANOTHER AJOR ATTACK AND E SENATE DECIDES TO RENEGE ON THE TREATY.
THERE WON'T BE ANY MORE ATTACKS. THINGS SHOULD QUIET DOWN NOW.
AND HOW DO YOU KNOW THAT?

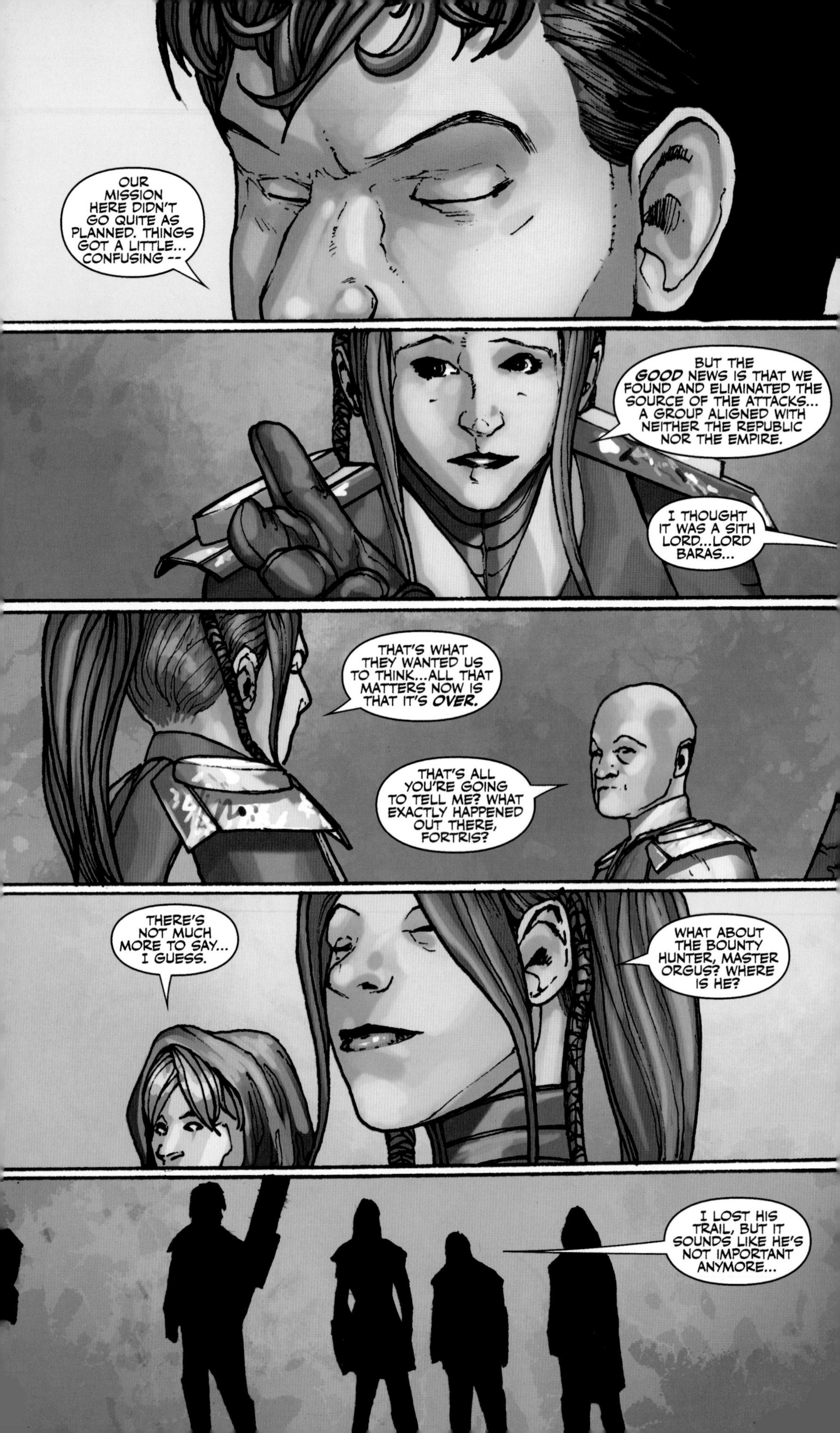
OUR MISSION HERE DIDN'T GO QUITE AS PLANNED. THINGS GOT A LITTLE... CONFUSING --
BUT THE GOOD NEWS IS THAT WE FOUND AND ELIMINATED THE SOURCE OF THE ATTACKS... A GROUP ALIGNED WITH NEITHER THE REPUBLIC NOR THE EMPIRE.
I THOUGHT IT WAS A SITH LORD...LORD BARAS...
THAT'S WHAT THEY WANTED US TO THINK...ALL THAT MATTERS NOW IS THAT IT'S OVER.
THAT'S ALL YOU'RE GOING TO TELL ME? WHAT EXACTLY HAPPENED OUT THERE, FORTRIS?
THERE'S NOT MUCH MORE TO SAY... I GUESS.
WHAT ABOUT THE BOUNTY HUNTER, MASTER ORGUS? WHERE IS HE?
I LOST HIS TRAIL, BUT IT SOUNDS LIKE HE'S NOT IMPORTANT ANYMORE...

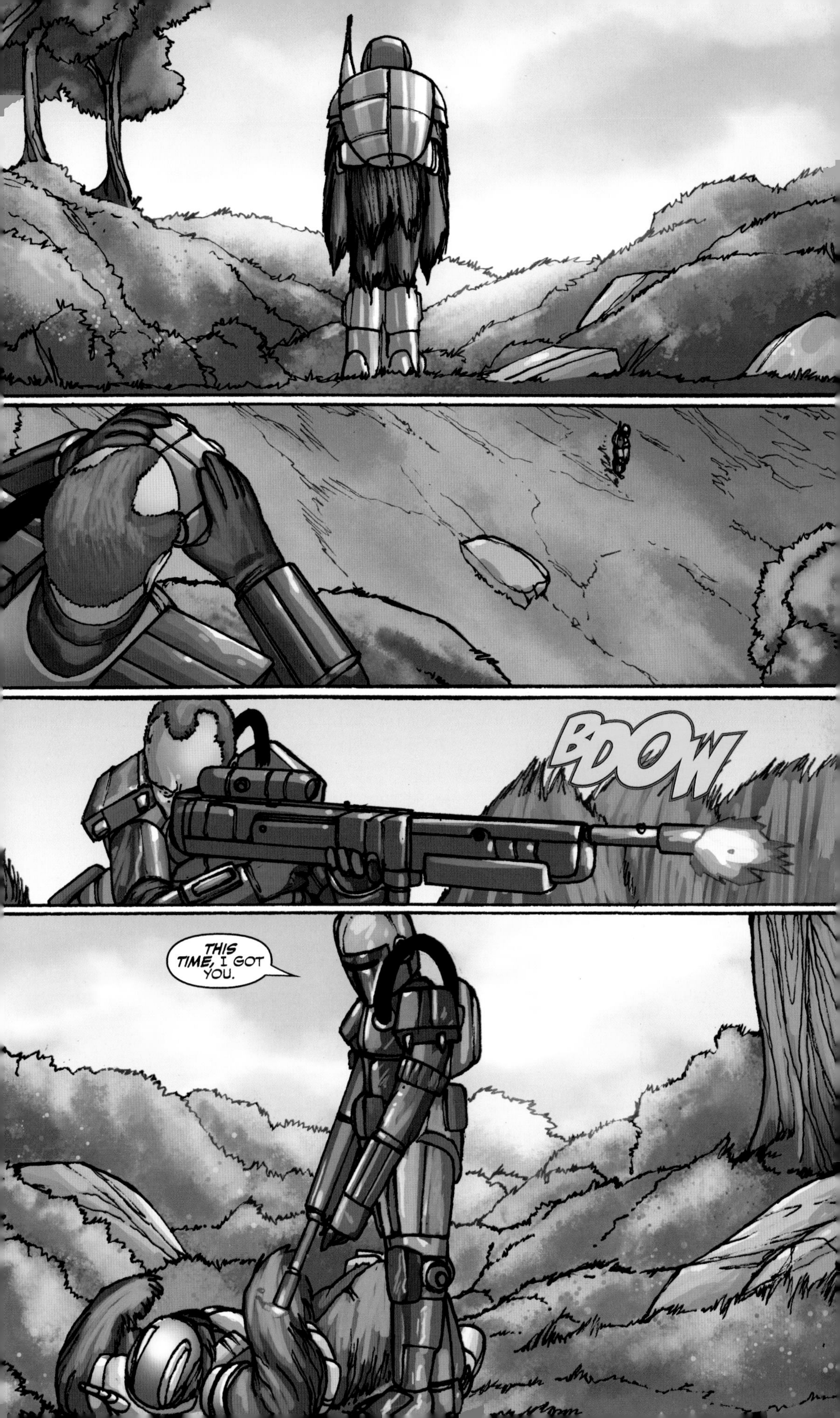
BDOW
THIS TIME, I GOT YOU.

NOTES OF
THE OLD REPUBLIC

BY ROB CHESTNEY

CORUSCANT

The Sacking of Coruscant is one of the most pivotal events in the Old Republic time period. The treaty signed by the Republic and the Empire after this event is absolutely preposterous. The Sith and the Jedi at peace? No way. It's this bizarre turn of events that *Threat of Peace* aims to explain. Hopefully, readers will come away with some understanding of why the Empire proposed such a treaty, why the Republic agreed to it, and why it presented such a struggle for the Jedi Order.

In the comic, readers see the Sacking of Coruscant firsthand, as Tavus and Orgus make a futile attempt to defend the planet. The Imperials seize and control the upper levels of Coruscant, driving Tavus, Orgus, and countless others into the lower levels. Given an extended occupation, these holdouts would have banded together and driven the Imperials off Coruscant, but the Sith knew the reality—they only planned to hold the planet long enough to secure the treaty.

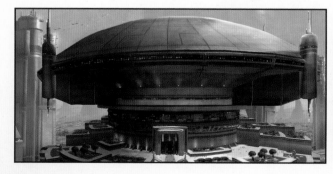 

Ultimately, the destruction on Coruscant, though considerable, was not catastrophic. Years later, much of the upper levels has been repaired. Some damage is still evident, but credits have been spent to make the face of the Republic as impressive as it ever was. The exception is the ruins of the Jedi Temple—an isolated eyesore that serves as a constant monument to the Sith assault.

ALDERAAN

Historically, Coruscant has always been the heart of the Republic, but Alderaan has been its soul. The beauty and nobility of Alderaan have made it the paragon of planets. In the years before *Threat of Peace*, however, Alderaan's tranquility was shattered when the Sith Empire invaded. A handful of Jedi and Republic Special Forces heroically defended the planet, making it a major victory for the Republic. Nonetheless, the Imperial attack was not forgotten. A few years later, the significance of holding the peace talks on Alderaan was lost on neither party.

After the Sacking of Coruscant, as seen in the comic, the Republic reluctantly agreed to the Empire's terms and signed the Treaty of Coruscant on Alderaan. Ironically, because of the lingering anger over the Imperial invasion, Alderaan later joins many other planets in withdrawing from the Galactic Senate.

NAR SHADDAA

Nar Shaddaa is probably the busiest place in the galaxy during the Old Republic time period. Governed in the loosest of terms by the Hutt crime cartels, the "smugglers' moon" is one of the few neutral places in the galaxy. Add to that a massive black market where advanced technology and all manner of contraband is traded, and it's clear why smugglers, pirates, and bounty hunters often consider Nar Shaddaa to be their home.

Despite the moon's neutrality, there are tensions between Imperial and Republic influences. Both sides would enjoy the Hutts' backing, but any overt attempts to force compliance would get messy and likely backfire. Behind the scenes, however, both sides are jockeying for the crime cartels' support, and there's no shortage of espionage and intrigue on Nar Shaddaa.

KORRIBAN

Recapturing their ancient homeworld was one of the Sith's first priorities when they returned from exile. The red rock planet bears witness to the glory and power of their ancestors. Sith and Imperial leaders govern the Empire from their Deep Space capital on Dromund Kaas, but the Sith Lords come to Korriban to experiment, conspire, and simply bask in the dark power that pervades the planet.

Lords Baras and Angral return to Korriban to receive their accolades from the Dark Council for a job well done after the attack on Coruscant. The brief clash between Baras and Angral is typical of the Sith Academy's atmosphere. The pretense of order exists on an official level, but anything goes when no one is watching. The lethal politics of the Sith breeds guarded secrets and ambiguous alliances.

BALMORRA

Battle rages across the cold, craggy terrain of Balmorra for almost the entire Old Republic time period. The planet's weapons- and droid-development facilities have been a target for the Empire since early in the war. Though Balmorra always maintained its independence, the planet's corporate leaders requested and received Republic military support when the Sith attacked. In the Treaty of Coruscant, though, the Republic agreed to withdraw.

In *Threat of Peace*, the seeds of an organized resistance to the Imperial occupation are sown in the defiance of Jedi Knight Fortris Gall. When the treaty is announced, Fortris's first concern is to free Republic prisoners of war before the withdrawal begins. His intentions are good, if not noble, but they influence the troops, who soon decide they're unwilling to withdraw. The Republic eventually disavows the stragglers, and they become an independent guerrilla resistance.

JEDI KNIGHT SATELE SHAN

Satele Shan is Bastila Shan's descendant. Bastila was a famous Jedi Master known for her "battle meditation" ability and saving the galaxy from Darth Malak. Satele has a lot to live up to, and from the start, she's beset with obstacles that threaten to drag her down. From her muddled foresight, to her overbearing Master, Satele's path is never easy. When a friendly flirtation begins with Lieutenant Tavus, it looks like she's headed towards a disconcerting romance, but this proves not to be the case. No matter how charming Tavus might be, Satele's dealing with issues that could mean the end of the Republic—she can't afford to lose perspective.

What's great about Satele is that she has the emotions, but she makes the right choices anyway. In the climax of *Threat of Peace*, Satele is confronted with the paradox of the peace treaty—how can the Jedi accept peace with enemies who are inherently violent and evil? Making her decision twice as hard, both her Master and Tavus have already given in to their anger. Satele's first instinct is to join them, but her commitment to what's right—standing for peace—actually wins out.

The traits we see in Satele here later earn her the honor of becoming Grand Master of the Jedi Order. In fact, Satele becomes one of the youngest Jedi in history to be given that esteemed position, but as she states in the comic, defeating the Sith is not her destiny, and she accepts that.

LORD BARAS

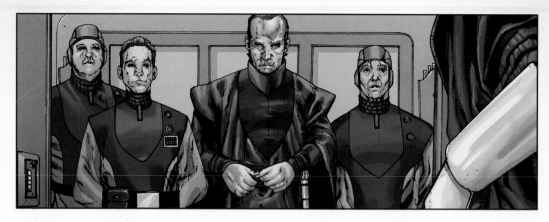

Rather than hatred and vitriol, Baras represents the more diabolical allure of the dark side. He's calm, controlled, and extremely reasonable, not a maniacal, evil Dark Lord. On Alderaan, Baras maintains perfect composure under pressure. Unlike Angral, Baras doesn't seethe with anger at the sight of a Jedi. His desire for vengeance against the Jedi is strong, but Baras sees the bigger picture. He's playing to win the war; the outcome of any single battle is not necessarily important.

The truth that's revealed later, of course, is that Baras is aware of one of the treaty's more sinister purposes—to confound and corrupt the Jedi, and specifically Satele Shan. Satele's name and her abilities make her the most prominent individual threat to the Empire during this time. If Baras can turn Satele to the dark side, not only does he strike a blow for the Empire, but he also acquires a powerful personal ally.

Despite Baras's strength in the Force and his skillful political maneuvering, we see a surprising twist on his character when he refuses the opportunity dangled in front of him by the Dark Council. Baras is a team player, but he thinks for himself and clearly has unconventional plans to realize his personal goals. For reasons that are not yet revealed, he deems it wiser to keep himself out of the spotlight at the present moment.

Ultimately, although Baras doesn't succeed in corrupting Satele Shan, his corrupting influence is in play on several fronts, and after the comic is concluded, his tendrils continue to spread through the Sith political structure. Rest assured; some day Baras will make his move. Only then will the true extent of his ambitions be revealed.

LIEUTENANT TAVUS

In *Threat of Peace*, Tavus represents the attitude of the Republic military and, to a lesser degree, that of the average Republic citizen. That's not to say Tavus is an average soldier—he's not. Orgus treats Tavus as an equal for a reason—he's an elite warrior and a natural leader. It's Tavus's attitude that's more representative of the military masses. Tavus's reaction to the peace treaty is skeptical from the start, and he quickly becomes one of the more vocal critics of the peace. Despite his personal assessment, Tavus follows orders like a good soldier. That is, until he meets more and more soldiers taking a stand, and the evidence piles up that the treaty is doomed. Then, Tavus decides to go with his gut, even at the cost of his romantic ambitions with Satele.

When he shoots the hapless protocol droid SP-99, Tavus has truly turned, and when Fortris and Dar'Nala request his assistance in attacking the Sith, any questions about Tavus's intentions are settled. Though Satele later brings Tavus back to the "right" side, we never see any evidence of Tavus having remorse for his actions. That's not to say that Tavus is wrong, necessarily. In fact, my hope is that readers actually sympathize with Tavus and walk away with mixed feelings.

Over the next several years, Tavus's career takes several turns. With the Jedi putting a little distance between the Order and the Republic, troopers like Tavus become the Republic's first line of defense. Tavus's heroics earn him the opportunity for promotion to a leadership position, but he chooses a role that keeps him on the front lines. His taste of politics after the Treaty of Coruscant is enough to convince him of where he truly belongs.

Jedi Master Orgus Din

Orgus is the kind of Jedi who was recruited to the Order with some doubt. Sure, he had Force potential, but his aptitude was limited. While other Padawans were breezing through their lessons, Orgus had to work twice as hard, especially to master the more obscure arts. To make up for this, Orgus drilled his lightsaber techniques endlessly, making himself one of the most respected duelists in the Order.

In the war, Orgus gravitated to a position working closely with the Republic military, fighting battles on border worlds across the galaxy. The Sacking of Coruscant really gets to him, though. He handles it well, but Orgus is deeply affected by the destruction of the Jedi Temple. That and the unfinished showdown with Angral will haunt Orgus over the next several years. If the two of them ever cross sabers again, only one will walk away.

Lord Angral

Angral is not just a Sith Lord; he's a Sith warlord. He embodies the anger, vengefulness, and ruthlessness expressed in the Sith philosophy. He's also disloyal, hotheaded, and arrogant, which will forever keep him from attaining a position within the Sith's inner circles of power. Angral doesn't care, though. He has a single-minded focus on the destruction of the Republic and the Jedi, and to achieve that is his highest ambition.

Though he plays by the rules set forth by the Dark Council, Angral will push those rules as far as he can go toward his vengeful aims. Rather than questioning the Dark Council's orders, he vents his frustration against Baras for not giving him more time on Coruscant. Angral will never defy the will of the Dark Council outright, but he will probably seize any opportunity to strike against the Republic if he has justified provocation.

BRADEN

Gutsy but practical, Braden has made a name for himself doing jobs for both sides during the war. He's not completely mercenary—he does have his own set of rules—but he earns his living the best way he knows how. At the opening of *Threat of Peace*, Braden is working for the Republic, but we quickly see why this relationship is problematic. A bounty hunter only owes loyalty to whoever is offering the credits, and the Republic can be a little squeamish. This is why the Empire is really a much better client for the bounty hunter's style of business.

Though he eventually gets his prize, Braden winds up a fugitive of both the Empire and the Republic. That's not a completely untenable position, but it certainly cuts down the number of available contracts. Over the next several years, Braden adapts, creating new strategies for generating wealth.

NOK DRAYEN

Nok Drayen's role in *Threat of Peace* is minimal, but he gives readers a good glance into the state of the galaxy's criminal underworld during the Old Republic time period. After decades of war, the Republic is a mess. The Empire, though dominant, is also strained to its limits, trying to manage all the star systems that have fallen into its dominion. The underworld, meanwhile, is prospering madly. From performing unsavory tasks for the two superpowers to flooding the black market with stims and implants, business has never been better. Crime lords like Nok Drayen are living large.

Nok himself, however, has a secret. The rationale for his partnership with Angral is left unexplored in *Threat of Peace*, but he has a strong personal motivation for the arrangement. Nok drops off the radar over the next several years on Nar Shaddaa, but he's far from out of the picture.